THE SHAPE OF THE TABLE

DAVID EDGAR

David Edgar was born in Birmingham in 1948 into a theatrical family. His stage plays include *Excuses Excuses* (Belgrade Theatre, Coventry, 1972), *Death Story* (Birmingham Repertory Theatre, 1972), *Dick Deterred* (Bush Theatre, London, 1974), *O Fair Jerusalem* (Birmingham Repertory Theatre, 1975), *Saigon Rose* (Traverse Theatre, Edinburgh, 1976), *Wreckers* (7:84 theatre company, 1977), *Our Own People* (Pirate Jenny theatre company, 1977), *Mary Barnes* (Birmingham Repertory Theatre then the Royal Court, London, 1978-9), *Teendreams* (with Susan Todd, Monstrous Regiment theatre company, 1979), *Entertaining Strangers* (Dorchester Community Play, 1985, National Theatre, 1987) and *That Summer* (Hampstead Theatre, London, 1987).

For the Royal Shakespeare Company he wrote *Destiny* (Other Place, Stratford, 1976; Aldwych Theatre, London, 1977), *The Jail Diary of Albie Sachs* (Warehouse Theatre, London, 1978), an adaptation of *Nicholas Nickleby* (Aldwych, 1980; Plymouth Theatre, New York, 1981) and *Maydays* (Barbican Theatre, London, 1983).

David Edgar is the author of several television plays, most recently, the three-parter *Vote for Them* (written with Neil Grant, and broadcast on BBC2 in June 1989). He also wrote the radio play *Ecclesiastes* (BBC, 1977), and the film *Lady Jane*. A volume of short plays, entitled *Edgar: Shorts*, was published in 1989. He is chair of Britain's first MA course in playwriting, which began in autumn 1989 at Birmingham University.

by the same author

Destiny
Entertaining Strangers
The Jail Diary of Albie Sachs
Mary Barnes
Nicholas Nickleby
Teendreams & Our Own People
That Summer
Wreckers
Vote for Them

Edgar Plays: One (*Destiny, Mary Barnes, The Jail Diary of Albie Sachs,
     Saigon Rose, O Fair Jerusalem*)
Edgar Plays: Two (*Ecclesiastes, Nicholas Nickleby, Entertaining Strangers*)
Edgar: Shorts (*Blood Sports* with *Ball Boys, Baby Love, The National
     Theatre, The Midas Connection*)

The Second Time as Farce

DAVID EDGAR

THE SHAPE OF THE TABLE

NICK HERN BOOKS

To Mike Newell and Bernice Stegers

A Nick Hern Book

The Shape of the Table first published in 1990 as a paperback original by Nick Hern Books, 31 Priory Road, Chiswick, London W4 5JA

The Shape of the Table copyright © 1990 by David Edgar
Cover image by Tim Moore © Royal National Theatre, London

Typeset and printed and bound by Expression Printers Limited, London N7 9DP

A CIP catalogue record for this book is available from the British Library

ISBN 1 85459 079 0

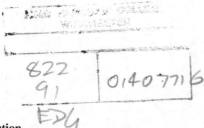
Caution
All rights whatsoever in this play are strictly reserved. Requests to reproduce the play in whole or in part should be addressed to the publisher. Applications for performance in any medium or for translation into any language should be addressed to the author's sole agent, Michael Imison Playwrights Limited, 28 Almeida Street, London N1 1TD.

Characters

Pavel PRUS, *writer, early 40s*
Monica FREIE, *administrative assistant, 20s*
Petr VLADISLAV, *minister of communications, late 30s*
Josef LUTZ, *first secretary of the Communist Party, early 60s*
Michal KAPLAN, *prime minister, late 50s*
Jan MILEV, *secretary of trade unions, mid–40s*
Vera ROUSOVA, *coalition party deputy, mid–50s*
Jan MATKOVIC, *Catholic intellectual, middle-aged*
Andrei ZIETEK, *student leader, early 20s*
Victoria BRODSKAYA, *opposition secretary, 21*
Victor SPASSOV, *former First Secretary, early 60s*

Other negotiators, including a Minister of Defence, a Bishop, a Social Democrat, and a Youth Leader.

Setting
The Banqueting Hall of a baroque palace in an Eastern European country, now used as a meeting room by the Communist government. There is a set of main double doors, and a smaller door leading to another room. There are windows. We can imagine we are on the first floor. The hall is dominated by a huge rectangular table, covered with a tablecloth, and surrounded by chairs. The play is set in late 1989.

The Shape of the Table was first staged in the Cottesloe by the National Theatre. First preview was 2 November 1990; first night was 8 November 1990.

The cast was as follows

PAVEL PRUS	Karl Johnson
MONICA FREIE	Hilary Lyon
PETR VLADISLAV	Stephen Boxer
JOSEF LUTZ	Stratford Johns
MICHAL KAPLAN	Oliver Ford Davies
JAN MILEV	Peter Sproule
VERA ROUSOVA	Sheila Keith
ANDREI ZIETEK	Andrew Woodall
JAN MATKOVIC	Christopher Ettridge
VICTORIA BRODSKAYA	Katrin Cartlidge
VICTOR SPASSOV	John Ringham
BISHOP	Alan Brown
SOCIAL DEMOCRAT	Peter Silverleaf
YOUTH LEADER	Jacqueline Dutoit
MINISTER OF DEFENCE	Harry Perscy

Directed by Jenny Killick
Designed by Dermot Hayes
Lighting by Paul Pyant
Music by Ian Dearden

Research by Nick Drake
Production Manager Jason Barnes
Stage Manager Trish Montemuro
Deputy Stage Manager Angela Fairclough
Assistant Stage Managers Valerie Fox, Andrew Speed
Sound Chris Johns
Assistant to the Lighting Designer Ian Williams
Design Assistant Miles King
Costume Supervisor Christine Rowland

ACT ONE

Scene One

Daytime. Both doors and the windows are closed. PAVEL PRUS *sits at one end of the long table. He is in his early 40s, with close-cropped hair, wearing a shabby suit and someone else's tie. After a few moments, he stands, goes to the window, looks out of it. He turns back, goes to the table, sits again. He is bored and annoyed. He stands and goes to the window again. Suddenly, a key turns in one of the main doors, they fly open and we hear a metallic clatter.* PRUS *turns to the noise in some alarm.* MONICA FREIE *pushes in a trolley full of bottles of soda water, fizzy drinks, glasses and bottle openers. There is also a notepad, with* FREIE's *orders for the day.* FREIE *is neatly dressed and in her 20s.*

PRUS. Hallo.

FREIE. Uh? Oh. Hallo.

PRUS. I'm sorry, I -

FREIE. No, no. I'm sorry I -

PRUS. Please. Please. It doesn't matter.

> FREIE *looks at the door she's just come through with its hanging keys. Then she looks at the other door.*

FREIE. Right.

> *She starts to set out fizzy drinks, soda water, glasses and openers in little clusters around the table.*

It's not usual for people to be early.

PRUS. Isn't it?

FREIE (*a joke*). Despite the resolution of the Fourteenth Congress.

PRUS (*responding*). Right.

> *She works on for a moment or two.*

FREIE. I haven't seen you here before.

PRUS. No. Well . . .

FREIE. New member?

PRUS. Not exactly.

FREIE. A co-opted expert.

PRUS. In a sense.

FREIE. A sense.

She decides to check the other door. She wheels the trolley down to it.

Of course, you could say that the Fourteenth Congress resolution just applied to promptitude at party meetings. But you could argue it should equally apply –

She's reached the other door, tests the handle, and finds it's locked.

– to any meeting a party person happens to attend. Who are you?

PRUS *stands.*

PRUS. Do you mean –

FREIE. I mean, what are you?

PRUS. By profession?

She shrugs 'yes'.

I'm a window cleaner.

FREIE. Window cleaner.

PRUS. But before that I was a copy editor.

FREIE. A what?

PRUS. And before that I wrote books.

FREIE. And now?

PRUS. Now I'm an inmate of a first category Correctional Institution.

FREIE. Ah. Ah, right.

She doesn't know what to do, as PRUS moves a little way towards her.

PRUS. So who are you?

FREIE. Uh, do you mean – ?

PRUS. I mean your name.

FREIE. It's Monica. I mean, it's Freie.

PRUS. And you're a what, a waitress?

FREIE. I'm a second category assistant in the Governmental Secretariat.

PRUS. Aha.

He sits.

FREIE. So they just, uh, just brought you here.

PRUS. That's right.

FREIE. From the, um, the first category . . .

PRUS. . . . . correctional . . .

FREIE. For some interview, or something –

PRUS. Well, so I'd assumed.

FREIE. And sort of dumped you.

PRUS. Mm.

Pause. He looks at the open door.

In fact, I ought perhaps to make a run for it.

He leans back in his chair.

Or maybe not.

FREIE. Well, that's . . . that's a relief.

Pause. PRUS *stands, and starts to help her lay out the bottles.* FREIE *decides not to fight this.*

So, then. What did a charmer like you do, to end up in a Correctional Institution?

PRUS. Oh, long story.

FREIE. So don't tell it.

PRUS. First of all, you see, I used to write these books.

FREIE. It's not illegal to write books.

PRUS. Of course not. But I found it harder and harder to get them published.

FREIE. P'raps they weren't that good.

PRUS. And so to earn a living I became a copy editor with a publisher. Which to be honest I found rather tedious.

FREIE. Well, we can't always do exactly what we want.

PRUS. Oh, absolutely not. And in fact I cheered up quite considerably when I was asked to compile a new anthology of children's fairy tales.

FREIE. So I should think.

PRUS. Especially when I started to get into it and realised how many themes these stories have in common, and how relevant those themes are to our situation now.

FREIE (*warily*). Go on.

PRUS. Well, almost all fairy-tales begin by establishing that the story is set a long time ago, far away, and in a time of particular and now lost possibilities. 'Once upon a time'. 'A thousand years ago or longer'. 'At a time when animals still talked'. 'In olden times when wishing still helped'.

FREIE. But they don't all end the same.

PRUS. Well, you say that. But they almost all have happy endings. 'They lived happily ever after'. 'And then all worries ended and they lived in perfect joy'. 'And so the bell rang and that's the end of the story'.

FREIE. Why shouldn't things end happily?

PRUS. No reason. I just think it's interesting all fairy stories do. As it's interesting that so many are about a good ruler dying, or being overthrown, and there being a contest for the succession. And there's sometimes people who look kind and nice and caring but who turn out to be monsters. And there may be a forbidden room, with a secret book, which will tell you everything, but if you read it may bring about what you least want, and leave you worse off than you were before. But at the end the false prince is exposed and punished, and the real prince comes into his kingdom. And I compiled a book of stories with those themes and they wouldn't publish them and when I asked why not they sacked me and so I became a gardener, a bricklayer and eventually a window-cleaner and I wrote a pamphlet about what I think the fairy tales are actually about and I ended up in jail for disseminating fabrications hostile to the state.

Pause.

I can't imagine why.

FREIE. You're Pavel Prus.

PRUS. That's right.

FREIE. The bombastic counter-revolutionary egoist.

PRUS. That's right.

PETR VLADISLAV *stands in the open doorway. He is bespectacled, suited, in his late 30s but looking younger. He carries a file.*

VLADISLAV. Please, what is going on?

FREIE. Ah. Comrade Minister. This is, well, um –

VLADISLAV. Yes, Comrade. I'm aware of who this is. What's this?

FREIE *takes her notepad from the trolley.*

FREIE. I am instructed to prepare the Great Hall of the 23rd of May for a 16.30 Plenum of the Ministerial –

VLADISLAV. A plenum?

He takes her notepad.

No, it's not a plenum. There's a meeting of the 18th of November working group, but that's upstairs, presumably. In that odd L-shaped arrangement off the gallery.

FREIE. The March the 10th suite.

VLADISLAV. Yes.

FREIE. But Comrade Minister -

VLADISLAV (*handing her the notepad*). Don't worry, comrade. Not your fault. A procedural irregularity. But you'd better leave this now.

FREIE *takes out her trolley.*

Mr Prus. I'm sorry you've been left so long.

PRUS. Another procedural irregularity?

VLADISLAV *looks at him.*

VLADISLAV. Yes, if you like. Do you want a soda water?

PRUS. Yes, why not.

VLADISLAV *opens two soda waters.*

VLADISLAV. My name is Vladislav.

VLADISLAV *hands a soda water to* PRUS *who pours it in a glass.*

PRUS. I know. You're the Deputy Minister of the Interior. And candidate member of the Politburo.

VLADISLAV (*sits*). Full member, actually. And as of August, Minister of Communications.

PRUS (*sits*). Oh, I beg your pardon.

VLADISLAV (*opening his file*). Don't apologise. It must be hard to keep on top of things.

PRUS. Yes, well.

VLADISLAV *reads from the file, with the odd glance at* PRUS.

VLADISLAV. 'As ever the worst thing is the isolation. I feel as if my head is in a plastic bag. I can hear the outside world and sense its shape but it's all muffled. Do not however try to send me news in letters as they will be stopped and as it is I still don't hear enough from you. Last night we watched a Polish film but of course they switched it off before the news. The film had very pretty girls, which made up for the dialogue'.

He looks at PRUS, *then turns to another section of the file.*

'My darling. Thank you for your last three letters, which arrived bunched up like trams. A benefit performance in the Hague was held for you. There were a dozen bands including Oedipus and People's Chemistry and the whole thing was apparently far out.

A look to PRUS.

'As well as raising over – blanked out – dollars.'

He shows it to PRUS.

PRUS. Well, it's obviously five figures.

VLADISLAV (*impressed*). Hm.

Turning to another section.

'Dear Anya. More and more, I feel that I am actually inside a fairy story, a land where everything is possible because nothing's what it seems. Please write as soon as maybe, certainly before the visit and if there's a chance of Dunhill International they're best but if not Marlboro will do.'

Pause.

PRUS. It's like in hospital. One has no control over one's circumstances. One becomes a child.

VLADISLAV. Well, yes. But I imagine that the most frustrating thing is not so much to get a letter with the best bits censored, but not knowing if there's things that haven't got to you at all.

He lays a typewritten airmail letter on the table. PRUS *picks it up.*

It's from the University of Illinois. A six month residency in the

Faculty of Languages. All expenses paid. And a stipend in I think five figures too.

PRUS *puts the letter down.*

PRUS. Well, what a pity. I'm in jail. And the DNS have got my passport.

VLADISLAV *takes a passport from his pocket and places it on the table.*

VLADISLAV. Well, we've agreed you're out of touch.

PRUS *looks at the passport.*

One of the other bits of news you may have missed is that there's been a certain streamlining of some administrative formalities. Visa applications for example. Sometimes it seems that they're approved before one's even got round to applying.

Pause.

PRUS. What's going on?

VLADISLAV. What, here?

PRUS. Outside.

VLADISLAV. Well, naturally, all-round socialist development continues. Cadres strive to implement the social goals set by the 14th Congress of the Party. Certain contradictions have emerged in certain sectors of our national life. Our gymnastic team continues to improve. We have qualified for the World Cup.

PRUS. What contradictions. In what sectors.

VLADISLAV. There have been, disturbances. Some larger cities.

PRUS. Demonstrations.

VLADISLAV. Hardly.

PRUS. Led by whom?

VLADISLAV. Oh, riff-raff. Anti-social elements.

PRUS. With what demands?

VLADISLAV. Largely provocative. Those that were not entirely specious we are looking at. For example, foreign travel. And a so-called amnesty for so-called political detainees.

PRUS. How big?

VLADISLAV. Oh, very small. We have so few.

PRUS. The demonstrations.

VLADISLAV. Big enough.

Slight pause.

And as you know full well, next Saturday's Republic Day. It's feared reactionary demagogues may pose a threat to public order.

PRUS. What, by pointing out Republic Day commemorates a putsch.

VLADISLAV. Whereas in fact of course it marks the founding of our socialist democracy.

PRUS. Why me?

VLADISLAV. What do you mean?

Slight pause.

PRUS. Last week I was described as an irrelevance. A self-advertising nobody. By your Prime Minister.

VLADISLAV. By *the* Prime Minister. I thought you didn't see the papers.

PRUS. That they showed me.

VLADISLAV. As I said, the contradictions in our national life have sharpened somewhat. Since last week.

PRUS *tosses the passport back on the table. Pause.*

It was felt you might care to delay your trip to Illinois. In order to participate more fully in the resolution of these contradictions.

PRUS. So then, what's the deal.

VLADISLAV. There is no deal. You write a single sentence letter, asking for a pardon.

PRUS. That's a deal.

Slight pause. VLADISLAV *puts a piece of paper on the table.*

VLADISLAV. You can re-phrase it if you like. After all, you are a literary man.

PRUS. My speciality is fairy stories, Mr Vladislav.

VLADISLAV *looks at* PRUS. *Then, briskly, tidying up his papers.*

VLADISLAV. Well, think about it, anyway.

PRUS. Look, can I have a cigarette?

VLADISLAV. Of course. Uh . . . Yes.

He goes to the door and calls.

Uh, comrade – comrade . . .

PRUS. Her name is Freie.

VLADISLAV. Uh, Comrade Freie!

FREIE appears.

FREIE. Yes, Comrade Minister?

VLADISLAV. D'you smoke?

FREIE. Yes, I'm afraid so.

VLADISLAV nods to PRUS. FREIE offers PRUS a cigarette.

PRUS. Thank you.

VLADISLAV nods again. FREIE leaves the packet and makes to go. PRUS puts the cigarette down on the table.

VLADISLAV. They're not your brand?

PRUS. I need a light. For some unfathomable reason . . .

VLADISLAV. Comrade, do you have a match?

FREIE puts a box of matches on the table and goes out. PRUS lights a match and sets fire to the draft letter as:

You see, it is entirely possible, that demands which presently appear . . .

PRUS lights his cigarette with the document. Then he puts it out in his soda water.

Oh, come, now. This is just a spectacle.

PRUS stands, goes to the window.

PRUS. Talking of spectacles, I've been observing your photographer. I can imagine, as we both emerge: 'The self-appointed bourgeois apologist Prus, justly imprisoned for the distribution of a hoarsely puerile and slanderous attack on the Republic, was today granted a free pardon by the Ministry of the Interior. Prus pleaded with the Ministry for his release on the grounds that it might contribute to preventing any escalation of the recent growth in public violence for which in part he must himself accept responsibility'.

Slight pause.

No. I should like to be released. But I shall leave from prison. On my own.

We hear the voice of JOSEF LUTZ, *approaching the main doors.*

LUTZ (*off*). In here?

FREIE (*off*). Uh, no. No, Comrade First Secretary. There's been a temporary shortcoming. The meeting is upstairs.

LUTZ *has entered, followed by* FREIE. *The First Secretary is in his early 60s. He sizes up the situation.*

LUTZ. Well, glory be.

Slight pause.

VLADISLAV. Comrade First Secretary. The prisoner . . .

LUTZ *gestures* FREIE *to go, and opens a fizzy drink.* FREIE *goes.*

LUTZ. You brought the prisoner here?

VLADISLAV. As was agreed.

LUTZ (*looking at the charred paper*). And still he turns you down?

LUTZ *goes to the telephone and dials.*

P. Prus. The famous and heroic 'dissident' who tugs the heartstrings of the New York Times with tales of how the wicked communists insist that people who live off the state should work for it. So different of course from how they do things in America.

PRUS. Yes, well, in America –

LUTZ (*down telephone*). Hallo. It's Lutz. I want to speak to the Prime Minister.
The Ambassador can wait.
The Hungarian Ambassador especially.
Well, will you tell him the First Secretary is in the 23 May now, and craves an audience.

He puts the phone down. To PRUS.

I'm sorry. You were saying. In America.

PRUS. In America the riot police don't beat up unarmed kids at concerts.

LUTZ. You are referring doubtless to last May's event in Friendship Park.

PRUS. Of course.

LUTZ. Which was if I may say 'a concert' in the sense that the Nazi burning of the books was a bonfire. Or the Night of the Long Knives a minor reconstruction of the Government.

PRUS. Or our showtrials here.

LUTZ (*joke*). Ah, but they were a minor reconstruction of the government.

PRUS. After which you spent four years in jail. As a Titoite conspirator, from 1952 –

LUTZ. Which is why you cut less ice with me, Prus, than you appear to with the Deputy Minister of the Interior.

Pause.

VLADISLAV. In fact . . .

LUTZ. Or whatever he's been elevated to.

Pause.

Well. We made our offer. You have turned it down. Definitively, it appears. I see no reason to prolong this conversation. You can go.

PRUS. Uh, do you mean?

LUTZ. Presumably there's somebody to take him back to jail?

VLADISLAV. Yes. Yes of course there is.

LUTZ. So there we are. All sorted.

He stands by the open door for PRUS. PRUS *pockets the cigarettes.*

PRUS. I came in handcuffs.

LUTZ. And you shall go back in them. And if you like, a set of irons and a ball and chain. Hey, you!

FREIE *appears.*

FREIE. Yes, Comrade Fir-

LUTZ. Will you deliver Mr Prus back to his escort. And you needn't worry. Mr Prus is a man of culture, delicacy and sophistication. Wouldn't hurt a fly.

PRUS *goes out with* FREIE. LUTZ *smiles, sits, and pats his pockets, looking for cigarettes.*

VLADISLAV. It is – I am the Minister of Communications.

LUTZ. Oh, yes. Of course. Promoted rather briskly, I remember. After that, unpleasant . . . Best thing, probably. D'you smoke?

VLADISLAV. No thank you.

He realises that wasn't what LUTZ was asking.

No, I don't. I'm sorry.

LUTZ. No. Of course.

The rattle of the small door being unlocked. Enter the Prime Minister, MICHAL KAPLAN. He's in his late 50s.

KAPLAN. First Secretary.

LUTZ. Prime Minister.

KAPLAN. Is this the meeting?

LUTZ. No. There's been a bureaucratic cock-up. It's upstairs.

KAPLAN (*to* VLADISLAV). And Prus?

During this LUTZ affects to read – and in doing so does read – PRUS' file.

VLADISLAV. He's gone, Prime Minister. He wouldn't sign.

KAPLAN. I see. So what should we do now?

VLADISLAV. I'd say we let him go. As a, humanitarian –

KAPLAN. Did he ask to be released?

VLADISLAV. Yes, in a way.

KAPLAN. In what way?

LUTZ. Well, it's obvious he's got your number, Vladislav.

VLADISLAV *and* KAPLAN *look at* LUTZ, *who points at a document in* PRUS' *file.*

Fairyland. 'Where everything is possible 'cos nothing's what it seems.' Well, glory be.

KAPLAN. You asked for me.

LUTZ. I did. I wanted to know the thinking of the government about the threat to public order on the 18th of November.

KAPLAN. There is a meeting. It's at 5.00 o'clock. In, I assume –

VLADISLAV. The 10th of March suite.

LUTZ. Yes, yes. This is the caucus.

Slight pause. KAPLAN *looks at his watch.*

Comrade Prime Minister. I am the First Secretary of the Party. I would like to know what's being planned to stop a rabble of provocateurs taking over People's Square on Saturday. What is going to be proposed at 5.00 o'clock.

KAPLAN. I believe the Minister of the Interior's presenting a report.

LUTZ. So, have you seen it?

KAPLAN. No.

LUTZ. Perhaps we might secure advanced sight of a copy.

VLADISLAV *goes to the phone.*

Of this no doubt top secret document.

Pause. KAPLAN *nods to* VLADISLAV, *to indicate that he should accept this humiliation.*

VLADISLAV. I'll see what I can do.

LUTZ. After all, you are the Minister of Communications.

VLADISLAV *goes out.* KAPLAN *sits and looks at* PRUS' *file.*

KAPLAN. You shouldn't underestimate him.

LUTZ. No? How old is he?

KAPLAN. Oh, certainly. You had indeed been several years a party member, and imprisoned by the fascist interlopers, and played your part in the establishment of socialism, with a little help of course from the Red Army, long before Petr Vladislav was thought of.

LUTZ. Hm.

KAPLAN. And even, just about, been slung in jail as a 'Trotskyite conspirator'.

LUTZ. It was – in the indictment – 'Titoite'.

KAPLAN. Well, yes.

LUTZ. And in 1960 I was rehabilitated.

KAPLAN. Very properly.

LUTZ. From which I learnt the Party can correct its own mistakes.

KAPLAN. From which you should perhaps have learnt that it is always a mistake to think that you can solve political problems by administrative means.

LUTZ. But as you well know, if I hadn't used 'administrative means' from time to time, then Victor Spassov would still have my job. And God knows who'd have yours. And I think we both know why we're in the party. Knowing just a little of what went before.

KAPLAN has gone back to looking at PRUS' *file.*

KAPLAN. Well. Yes.

LUTZ. Which is why, Michal, in present circumstances -

KAPLAN. Bells.

LUTZ. Beg pardon?

KAPLAN. It's the phrase, 'and so the bell rang and the story ends'. I'd never thought, why bells.

LUTZ. You what?

KAPLAN. I suppose it's the expression: 'the story isn't over till they ring the bell'.

LUTZ. Well, you know, I've really no idea.

KAPLAN (*looking up from the file*). Well, yes. Well, yes, indeed.

Enter VLADISLAV *with documents.*

VLADISLAV. Apparently, First Secretary, all this is on your desk.

He gives copies to LUTZ *and* KAPLAN.

KAPLAN. You've read it?

VLADISLAV. I have glanced at it.

LUTZ. Then why not summarize. As after all –

VLADISLAV. – I am the Minister of Communications. According to the DNS, there are likely to be demonstrations on the 18th of November in at least five cities, including here in the capital, where the marchers are expected to attempt to enter People's Square.

LUTZ. 'The marchers'. Led by whom?

VLADISLAV. My understanding is that thus far the um, disturbances, have been more or less spontaneous.

LUTZ. Comrade, you'll learn there's nothing needs more organising than a more or less spontaneous disturbance.

VLADISLAV. But insofar as they have been planned, the leadership has consisted of some former Party members, priests, a lot of students, particularly those studying artistic subjects, so-called dissidents, some workers in the entertainment industry, and environmental activists.

LUTZ. When you say former Party members?

VLADISLAV. Largely those active in the period of bourgeois restoration.

LUTZ. Superannunated Spassovites, in fact.

VLADISLAV. Well, if you like.

LUTZ. So 'former' in the sense of 'purged'?

VLADISLAV. Largely by you, First Secretary.

LUTZ. So to sum up, it's defeatist party has-beens, misfit riffraff, mystics, cranks, some failed theatricals and juvenile delinquents. What's the plan to sweep 'em off the streets?

VLADISLAV. The options are threefold. The first is to allow the demonstration to occur, and let it be and hope that it stays reasonably peaceful.

KAPLAN. And reasonably small.

VLADISLAV. Which will of course mean it'll be extensively reported on the radio.

LUTZ. Oh, will it now?

VLADISLAV. By the BBC, Voice of America, and other networks over which my Ministry does not have absolute control.

LUTZ. Could always jam 'em.

KAPLAN. Not to mention Western television.

VLADISLAV. Which will mean of course that the demonstrations will continue. And continue growing larger. The second option is to use the SDU to disperse the demonstrations, using the usual anti-riot methods.

LUTZ. Yes, go on?

VLADISLAV. And that is viewed as possible in the provincial cities where the demonstrations are indeed expected to be reasonably small. Here on the other hand the estimation is that we're talking 50,000. In which case, it's possible they might not be shifted. By watercannon, teargas and the like.

LUTZ. So then. The third alternative.

VLADISLAV. I'm not sure one can have a third alternative.

LUTZ. You take care, Vladislav.

   KAPLAN *frowns at* VLADISLAV.

VLADISLAV. The final option is not seen as thinkable.

KAPLAN. What is it, Petr?

VLADISLAV. Issuing live ammunition to the SDU.

   Pause.

LUTZ. So what's unthinkable about that?

   Slight pause.

VLADISLAV. The problem is apparently not so much the dead, as the
   seriously wounded. The calculation is, the first two volleys knock out
   up to 20, and seriously injure upwards of a hundred more. And of
   course there are field hospitals, at strategic points along the route
   and adjacent to the square. But even so, if a hundred plus are
   seriously injured at one time, the medical resources fail. Oh, and
   unless we're inconceivably fortunate with blood types, plasma starts
   to run out when we're much beyond that point. So really from about
   an hour in, it's our youth, the future of our country, bleeding
   literally to death, on world-wide satellite TV.

   Pause.

   I think the issue is, if the SDU could be prevailed upon to do that,
   comrades.

   Pause.

LUTZ. Well, that's most dramatic, but there is of course a Fourth
   Alternative.

KAPLAN. What's that?

LUTZ. I'm surprised it isn't listed. Used it once before.

VLADISLAV. You mean the Soviet –

LUTZ. I mean calling on our eastern ally for fraternal military
   assistance.

   Pause.

KAPLAN. Have they helped anybody else?

LUTZ. Has anybody asked?

VLADISLAV. Yes, actually they have. We have. As you would expect. As an academic question, naturally. Exploring the contingencies. With the military leaders of our great friend and neighbour.

LUTZ. And?

Slight pause.

VLADISLAV. The answer was quite clear.

LUTZ. Well, not to me.

VLADISLAV. It's up to us. We're on our own.

LUTZ. And, Comrade, may I ask, just how you know all this?

VLADISLAV. It's on page 12, First Secretary.

Slight pause.

LUTZ. I see.

KAPLAN. So what's he recommend?

VLADISLAV. He doesn't. It's an options paper.

LUTZ. Ha!

VLADISLAV. But for what it's worth, it seems to me . . .

LUTZ. Yes, yes? How does it seem to you?

VLADISLAV. That as we can't expect fraternal help, that it would be, statesmanlike of the First Secretary to persuade the Minister of the Interior against – the Tiananmen Alternative. But to call instead upon the forces of security to show the utmost vigilance in the preservation of the peace.

LUTZ. You mean, beat 'em up, not mow 'em down?

VLADISLAV. Well, that's a way of putting it, First Secretary.

Enter FREIE.

FREIE. Excuse me, Comrade. It's the Director of the Radio.

VLADISLAV. Oh, yes, of course. Forgive me.

VLADISLAV goes out, followed by FREIE. A pause.

KAPLAN. I told you, Josef.

LUTZ. Hm.

Slight pause. KAPLAN notices VLADISLAV has left PRUS' file. He picks it up.

Hey. You know what strikes me, reading all that shit? From Prus and all the other 'persecuted intellectuals'?

KAPLAN. No. What strikes you, Josef?

LUTZ. It's that fundamentally, deep down, they hate the working class. They think its tastes are crude. They don't like what it eats or drinks or does at night. They are affronted by its smell. They think it's thick. They regard themselves as several cuts above it in all things. While the one thing that you can say for the Spassovites, about the only thing in fact, is at least they didn't wrinkle up their noses at a sweaty armpit or a dirty fingernail.

KAPLAN. Yes, I sometimes think, what might have happened. If Victor Spassov had been just a little more discreet with his reforms. And our eastern neighbour just a little less – precipitate in his response to them.

Slight pause.

LUTZ. Michal. Victor Spassov was an opportunist and capitulationist who became First Secretary of the Party through unprincipled manipulation, and whose programme of so-called reform objectively amounted to the restoration of the bourgeosie. The working masses thus had cause to be particularly grateful for the military assistance requested and received from our fraternal ally to the east. As was agreed unanimously at the Special Congress of November 1970. To which as I recall you were a delegate.

KAPLAN. And at which you were appointed by the party to see to it that such aid would not be needed in the future.

LUTZ. I was appointed to consolidate the party. And as you well know, if the Spassovites had won, they'd have done for me every bit as quickly as I did for them.

Slight pause.

KAPLAN. Of course. And we must hope your work is still effective. In view of recent changes in the character of our great neighbour.

LUTZ *looks at* KAPLAN. *Collecting his papers:*

LUTZ. Well, I've just two things to say on that. The first is, that I see no reason, if your neighbour decorates his flat, for you to do the same.

KAPLAN (*with a little smile*). And, second?

LUTZ. I hope they get a damn good hiding.

LUTZ *goes out through the main doors.*

KAPLAN. Right.

Scene Two

A week later. VLADISLAV *is on the telephone, taking notes.*

VLADISLAV. I'm sorry, give me that again. How many?
    Then how many.
    So, um, could you . . .
    Yes, and *what.*
    Um, could you spell that?
    Oh, I see. And this was universal?
    No, yes. Yes. Well, thank you very much. Yes, please.

He puts the phone down. Enter KAPLAN *through the small door. He has a document file.*

KAPLAN. The First Secretary?

VLADISLAV. He's not arrived.

KAPLAN. Perhaps he's been held up in traffic.

VLADISLAV. Well, there is a lot of it about. But, look, apparently -

KAPLAN. As it happens, if he wasn't able to attend, he wouldn't be the only one.

VLADISLAV. Oh, yes?

The phone rings. VLADISLAV *answers.*

Yes, what?

To KAPLAN.

The NPP's here.

KAPLAN. Let them wait.

VLADISLAV (*down phone*). Please apologise and say we've been delayed.

He puts the phone down.

KAPLAN. After all, they're used to it.

VLADISLAV. Indeed.

KAPLAN. Now, you were saying.

VLADISLAV. So were you.

KAPLAN. Oh, yes. The thing is, that, unhappily -

Enter JOSEF LUTZ *and* JAN MILEV. MILEV *is in his mid–40s. He's the head of the Trade Unions.*

LUTZ. Well, glory be. Good morning, comrades.

VLADISLAV *looks at his watch.*

Oh, is it afternoon? How time flies, when one is in good company. Petr, you know the Chairman of the General Federation of Trade Unions?

VLADISLAV. Yes, obviously I know Comrade Milev.

LUTZ. Of course, of course. No doubt you have communicated on a wide variety of topics.

VLADISLAV. Good day, comrade.

MILEV. Comrade.

LUTZ. Well, we have spent the morning at a meeting at the 26th of February Auto Plant. It was most refreshing. As you can imagine, there were many arguments put forward, many views expressed. There was however a general consensus that the government should stand firm at all costs against the provocations of a tiny anti-communist minority endangering our continued socialist development. Would you not say, Jan?

MILEV. Yes, that was the general opinion.

LUTZ. They were particularly incensed by the way the malcontents incite the foreign media to slanderous attacks upon our country. They were particularly outraged by well-paid artists, actors and the like, the beneficiaries of our country's most enlightened cultural and education policies, manufacturing these lies and fabrications. They were peculiarly insistent that the security institutions should be fully backed as they set about the task of preserving the achievements of the working people and their government. And not be stabbed in the back.

MILEV. Yes, that view was hotly put.

VLADISLAV. Comrade Prime Minister, I trust the First Secretary made it clear that the Government does indeed support the police in their efforts in this difficult time. My own ministry, for example, saw to it that the First Secretary's opinions on the matter were given considerable prominence in all communications media. Particularly his unconditional support for the tactics of the Special Duties Unit on the night of the 18th, and his remark that it was high time that the juvenile delinquents on the street were given a good hiding. A remark that was indeed reported in the western media repeatedly.

LUTZ. I would remind the Minister that the tactics pursued on the 18th were his idea.

VLADISLAV. I won't remind the Secretary of what he had in mind.

MILEV. So what was that?

VLADISLAV. What I hear the SDU refers to as the Chopstick Option.

MILEV smiles.

LUTZ. And out of which the Minister had better not be thinking he might wriggle.

VLADISLAV. I think it was clear to everyone that the First Secretary was not amenable to any less aggressive tactics than the ones that were eventually employed. The issue was to stop us being shown on international television mowing our own people down.

Pause.

KAPLAN. Well, what was shown was hardly helpful to our international standing. And it failed to stop the demonstration. Or the demonstrations which have followed it.

Slight pause.

MILEV. The worst of both worlds, one might say.

KAPLAN. Yes, I suppose one might.

Slight pause. He looks at his watch.

Well, we are scheduled for a meeting of the working group to discuss proposals from the opposition.

LUTZ sits.

LUTZ. Oh. What oppositions this?

KAPLAN looking for a document in his file.

KAPLAN. I think they now call themselves the Public Programme.

LADISLAV. Platform.

KAPLAN (*finding the document*). Platform, yes. Unhappily, the Minister of the Interior is unable to be with us.

KAPLAN waits for MILEV to pick up that he should go.

Being the other member of this working group.

Slight pause.

MILEV (*making to go*). OK.

LUTZ. You stay here, Jan. I'm told by my informants – doubtless most inaccurate, they're in the secret police – that these bastards want to sell our industry to international speculators. Should be of interest to the leader of the independent organising body of the working class. I'd get your coat off and sit down.

Pause.

KAPLAN. Well, perhaps, as an observer . . .

MILEV, VLADISLAV *and* KAPLAN *sit.*

VLADISLAV. In fact, the proposal isn't so much about industry as about allowing a more flexible approach to the ownership of service enterprises. You know, like restaurants and garages and clothes shops and the like.

LUTZ. Oh, they concede the working class is up to running autoplants and steelworks?

VLADISLAV. I think they think it would be quite hard in their present state to find anyone to buy them.

Pause.

KAPLAN. This is the document. It is called 'For a New Dawn'.

LUTZ. New what?

VLADISLAV. It's a reference to the Spassov period. You may recall, he called his programme of reform 'New Morning'.

LUTZ. Programme of 'reform'?

VLADISLAV. I'm sorry. Bourgeois restoration.

LUTZ. Right.

KAPLAN. Well, whatever they or we might call it, in this document there are ten items. The first is the proposal for immediate talks with the present leaders of the country.

LUTZ. With the party.

KAPLAN. With the government.

LUTZ. The party has the leading role in our society. It's in the constitution.

KAPLAN. Yes. That's item two.

Slight pause. MILEV *whistles.*

I think the argument is that the party and the state should be distanced from each other. So. Item three is the involvement of what they describe as civil institutions in the talks. That's churches, other parties, youth . . .

MILEV. When they say 'other parties'? Do they mean new parties?

KAPLAN. I presume they mean our partners.

LUTZ. Oh, you mean the stooges.

KAPLAN. No, I mean the independent parties presently in voluntary coalition with us in the Patriotic Bloc.

MILEV. That's presently for 40 years.

LUTZ. And voluntary my arse.

KAPLAN *is getting riled by this.*

KAPLAN. Item four is amnesty for all politicals –

LUTZ. Already done.

VLADISLAV. Well partially.

LUTZ. Enough. Since you let him out, your Pavel Prus is hardly off the BBC, Im told.

VLADISLAV. It's not – my Pavel Prus.

LUTZ. And sadly, not your BBC.

KAPLAN. Item five is an investigation into the events of the 18th, and six is the immediate dismissal of all those responsible for violence against the demonstrators.

LUTZ (*with a look at* VLADISLAV). Aha.

MILEV. Not the violence against the police.

VLADISLAV. There was no violence against the police. What there was against the police was a line of children holding flowers and sparklers and I can't see that there's any point in this discussion if we don't accept that.

Pause.

LUTZ. And seven?

KAPLAN. Seven is the loosening of the economy, eight's legalising so-called free trade unions and parties, this isn't in any very rational order, nine's a commission to reassess the treatment of the Spassovites, and ten's their rehabilitation.

Slight pause.

Those two are obviously mutually dependent. In fact, it's a little prejudgmental having both.

LUTZ. Oh, yes. A little.

KAPLAN. So I'd imagine we'd have differences with number ten.

LUTZ. I'd imagine we'd have differences with numbers one to nine.

KAPLAN. But I think we should agree to talk with Public Platform, on the basis of this rough agenda. And that we put that as a proposition to the politburo.

Pause.

LUTZ. Michal, that's quite ridiculous. I couldn't put that to the politburo, or anybody else.

Slight pause.

KAPLAN. No. No, I see that. No, you couldn't, could you, really.

LUTZ. What?

Pause.

Oh no you don't.

VLADISLAV *reads from his notes.*

VLADISLAV. Comrade First Secretary. When you and Comrade Milev first arrived, you reported on your meeting at the 26th of February Auto Plant. I don't think that it was entirely accurate.

Slight pause.

MILEV. What do you mean?

VLADISLAV. I mean that there was no 'general consensus' around the opinions the First Secretary expressed. Indeed, that there was much support for talks with Public Platform. That when, comrade, you described the protestors as a bunch of malcontents, the workers shouted back 'we are all malcontented'. In the manner of a football chant. Which then developed into 'we're all juvenile delinquents' and 'Oh Joe, Oh Joe, it's time to go, so go Joe, so go'.

Slight pause.

LUTZ. Where did you hear this?

VLADISLAV. Oh, I have my sources. After all, I am the Minister of Communications.

Pause.

MILEV. Well, some people shouted things like that. Big meeting.

VLADISLAV. I am told that it was big. But not that it was some.

LUTZ *gestures to* KAPLAN.

LUTZ. Give me that list.

He takes the list.

OK, I'm not averse to talks. About the talks. And sure, why not, it's just accepting it as an agenda. The free union's a nonsense, it's an opposition front, but if they want the stooges let 'em have 'em. And if they want to rake up Spassov and the period of the consolidation, well, I've nothing I'm ashamed of.

KAPLAN. Josef, the problem isn't whether we accept the coalition parties, but their attitude to us. The social democrats are thinking of withdrawing from the coalition. The Catholics are printing opposition statements in their newspaper. I've got the National Peasants' Party in the lobby.

LUTZ. So now we take our orders from the National Peasants' Party?

VLADISLAV. And that's not to mention what we're hearing from inside our own.

LUTZ. Well, obviously there's class collaborationists and fainthearts on the fringes –

KAPLAN. Josef. The 26th of February Auto Plant is not the fringes of the party or the class.

Pause.

VLADISLAV. I should have added, that it was assumed, First Secretary, from your demeanour, you might be unwell.

Pause.

LUTZ. I see. And may I ask, has whatever bug I've got been picked up by the Minister of the Interior?

KAPLAN. I can say, confidentially, that the Minister has submitted his resignation. On the grounds of a persistent bronchial complaint.

MILEV. So who takes over?

KAPLAN. Well, it is of course not my decision –

LUTZ. Oh, come on.

KAPLAN. But I think I'd recommend the council to put Petr forward to the President.

LUTZ. Oh would you now.

VLADISLAV *is taken aback, and trying to suppress that and his delight.*

All right. I'll go.

KAPLAN. First Secretary, I'm absolutely sure –

LUTZ. On two conditions.

Slight pause.

KAPLAN. Yes?

LUTZ. One is, no shit about ill health. I've not jumped, I've been pushed.

KAPLAN. All right.

LUTZ. And two. I'll be demoted, but I won't be dumped. I want another job.

Pause.

KAPLAN. Go on.

LUTZ. My father was a metal worker. My first job for the party was a workplace organiser. That's how I started, that's how I'll end up.

VLADISLAV. As a workplace organiser?

MILEV. I think he means, as the Chairman of the General Federation of Trade Unions.

KAPLAN. I didn't know there was a vacancy.

MILEV. Neither did I. But I could use a change.

LUTZ. Well, excellent. And I understand we need a new Minister of Communications.

VLADISLAV. Over my –

LUTZ. Or else you could shift Ledl out, as I've been telling you for years, and give Jan Labour. Or whatever you've put with it now.

MILEV. Health and Social Welfare.

LUTZ. See? He's mastered the portfolio already.

KAPLAN. And you're happy with that, Jan?

MILEV. Gimme a Zil, delirious.

KAPLAN. So then, that's settled.

Pause. VLADISLAV *bites his lip.*

And I suppose I ought to see the NPP.

They all stand. VLADISLAV *goes out, to ask for the waiting person to be brought.*

LUTZ. So who d'you plan to put up for the talks?

KAPLAN. Oh, well, you know, I thought I'd volunteer myself.

LUTZ. With Vladislav.

KAPLAN. Yes, I'd thought, the Minister of the Interior.

LUTZ. Of course.

Reenter VLADISLAV.

VLADISLAV. He's on his way.

KAPLAN. It's she, in fact, I think.

LUTZ. Though I would have thought, as an addition, that one might consider that the Minister of Labour, Health and Social Welfare would make something of a contribution. To a meeting to negotiate the future of the party of the working class.

VLADISLAV. Um –

Enter MONICA FREIE.

FREIE. Comrade Prime Minister. It's Mrs V. Rousova to see you.

KAPLAN. Yes, please, show her in.

Exit FREIE.

LUTZ. I'm absolutely certain that the party leadership would take that view.

Re-enter FREIE *with* VERA ROUSOVA. *She is in her late 50s.*

Well, glory be. A National Peasant. I'll see you at the meeting, Michal.

LUTZ *and* MILEV *go out by the main doors.* LUTZ *has left a file behind.*

KAPLAN. Madame Rousova. How are you. Have you met Petr Vladislav?

ROUSOVA. No, not as such. How do you do.

She shakes VLADISLAV*'s hand.*

VLADISLAV. How do you do.

FREIE. And Comrade Minister, the Party Secretary for Agitation's waiting for you in your office.

VLADISLAV. Right. You will forgive me.

ROUSOVA. More readily I would imagine than your visitor.

VLADISLAV and FREIE go out.

KAPLAN. Madame Rousova, I am delighted you could come. Please do sit down. Can I offer you some coffee?

ROUSOVA sits.

ROUSOVA. No thank you. Your secretary has been most solicitious. I am awash with coffee.

KAPLAN. As are we with – carbonated drinks.

ROUSOVA. Well, Mr Kaplan. This is something of a first.

KAPLAN. What is?

ROUSOVA. Being called 'madame' by the leader of the Communists.

KAPLAN. Ah, sadly, you inflate my station. I am just Prime Minister.

ROUSOVA. That's what my father always said. It was a great annoyance to his colleagues in the Government.

KAPLAN. Whereas the only party leader present is yourself.

Slight pause.

ROUSOVA. What party's this?

KAPLAN. Your father's party.

ROUSOVA. Oh, Mr Kaplan, I have not been involved with the Peasants' Party now for many years.

KAPLAN. You are its Honorary President.

ROUSOVA. I am?

KAPLAN takes a letter from a file and places it before MRS ROUSOVA. She looks at the letterhead.

Well, so it would appear.

She reads the letter, as:

KAPLAN. This is a letter from the Peasants' Party leader in the National Assembly. I had approached him in the hope the Council of Ministers might be widened, to include some members of our coalition partner parties. This is his reply.

ROUSOVA. It seems entirely sensible.

KAPLAN. It's a prevarication.

ROUSOVA. Yes.

KAPLAN. We'd hoped for a more positive response.

ROUSOVA. Herr Rat inquires of Fraulein Flea if she'd like to join him for a swim.

KAPLAN. Now this is melodrama, Madame Rousova.

ROUSOVA. Mr Kaplan. 40 years ago, the leaders of your party faced the leaders of the Peasants' Party with a choice. It could either join the charade of the Patriotic Bloc, or suffer the same fate as the Smallholders, the Lutherans and the Revolutionary Socialists. In the latter case, I have to say, a fate richly deserved. Now having used us as a parliamentary rubber stamp for 40 years, you ask the party to participate in real power. Well, I wonder why.

KAPLAN. Our party is committed to the deepening of socialist democracy throughout society.

ROUSOVA. Your party is committed now to what our party was committed to in 1948. That's saving its own skin.

KAPLAN. Which is why steps have been taken to renew the party leadership. In order to avoid a repetition of past negative developments.

Pause.

ROUSOVA. I see.

KAPLAN. In order to enable the commencement of an even fuller dialogue.

ROUSOVA. You're going to talk to Public Platform?

KAPLAN. Yes.

ROUSOVA. Who else?

KAPLAN. It's hoped such talks will rapidly expand to include all social forces.

ROUSOVA. And what is the agenda for the talks?

KAPLAN. Oh, I think that that's a matter for the people at them.

ROUSOVA. Because I am informed the reason why the National Peasants' Party took the view it did, in 1948, is that despite its loathing of the communists and all they stood for – all you stand for – and despite the feeling that the country had been taken over by plebian thugs and cultureless barbarians, you were still after all the Government of what was after all our country. And that is why, despite the years of vulgar insults heaped upon the party and my father, the collaborationist, the fascist stalking horse, why it is so striking now to hear what are no more than children marching through the streets and calling out his name.

KAPLAN. I think . . . I'm sure that there has been . . . what one might describe as a dogmatic attitude to our country's post-war history.

ROUSOVA. And its pre-war history.

KAPLAN. Its history this century. And I am sure that it's a matter that will be freely and, um, positively addressed in the negotiations.

Pause.

ROUSOVA. Good.

KAPLAN. We were thinking that the NPP might consider taking the portfolios of Forestry and Agriculture.

ROUSOVA. Yes. Well, I am but an Honorary President.

KAPLAN. Of course.

ROUSOVA. But I will do my best.

She stands. A sudden thought.

Were there not mirrors in this room?

KAPLAN. Uh, mirrors?

ROUSOVA. Yes. I'm sure it was this room.

KAPLAN. Uh, what –

ROUSOVA. There was a supper. Well, a banquet, really. And I was only, what?, eleven at the time, but I was permitted to attend the first two courses of the eight or nine. And I remember raising up my spoon, and seeing my face in the mirror, with this – ladle at my lips, and thinking: I'm so glad I'm not outside.

LUTZ has re-entered.

LUTZ. So when was this? This glittering occasion?

Slight pause.

ROUSOVA. 1940. And stuffed with German dignitaries of course. Just a month before they declared martial law, dismissed the government, dissolved the party, rounded up 200 of its leaders and despatched them God knows where.

LUTZ. But not your dad.

ROUSOVA. No, not my father, no.

Slight pause.

Which I suppose explains why he didn't want to see the party banned again, in 1948. And you might think he was wise. Goodbye, Prime Minister.

She takes KAPLAN's hand.

KAPLAN. Goodbye.

He makes to lead her out.

ROUSOVA. Don't worry. I still know the way.

She goes out. Pause. There is a difficult moment between the two men.

LUTZ. So. Made your deal?

KAPLAN. We – had our conversation.

LUTZ. I forgot my file.

Slight pause.

KAPLAN. It's there.

Slight pause. LUTZ goes and picks up his file.

LUTZ. Well, glory be. Best part of 20 years.

KAPLAN. Yes, so it is.

Pause.

Look, Josef. No-one disagrees, that after Spassov, someone had to clean things up, consolidate the party. Save it from itself.

LUTZ. Oh, yes.

KAPLAN. In the same way, as I am determined that the party will survive this crisis, now. If not alone, then in partnership with others.

LUTZ. Hm.

KAPLAN. And if we have to change the colour-scheme, rehang the wallpaper, or even knock down and rebuild the walls, then I'm determined –

LUTZ. Shh.

KAPLAN. I'm sorry?

LUTZ. Shh. Do you not hear it? Kind of, ringing?

KAPLAN *listens.*

KAPLAN. No?

LUTZ. No more can I.

LUTZ *goes to the door. He grins at* KAPLAN.

So perhaps the story isn't over after all.

He goes out.

Scene Three

Next day. Around the table is the Public Platform group, led by PRUS. JAN MATKOVIC *is middle-aged,* ANDREI ZIETEK *is in his early 20s and the secretary,* VICTORIA BRODSKAYA, *is 21. There's a Western ghetto-blaster on the table.*

ZIETEK. So this is it?

MATKOVIC. I thought it was supposed to be informal.

PRUS. I'm not sure our view of what's 'informal' would quite match.

ZIETEK. Not sure our view of anything'll match.

PRUS. This is where they dumped me last time. It's the Great Hall of the 23rd of May.

ZIETEK. So what happened on the 23rd of May?

PRUS. Wasn't it the Adoption of the Constitution?

MATKOVIC. Ah, a literary commemoration.

ZIETEK. So does anybody want a pop?

MATKOVIC. Why not.

ZIETEK *pours fizzy drinks for* MATKOVIC, *and for* BRODSKAYA, *who nods that she'd like one.* PRUS *gestures not.*

PRUS. Apparently, in Moscow, if you've got a complaint, you go to the Great Hall of the Praesidium. And you wait for ages and eventually you see a grey man sitting in a little booth. And you tell him about your complaint. And they note it carefully, and then they put you in a mental hospital.

MATKOVIC. Or did.

ZIETEK. Now they make you Editor of Pravda.

PRUS. But only if you're genuinely crazy. Well, while we're waiting . . . Vicky, do you have the draft?

BRODSKAYA. Yes, Mr Prus.

As BRODSKAYA *gives* PRUS *a document,* ZIETEK *produces a bag of fruit.*

ZIETEK. Oh, and does anybody want a tangerine?

PRUS. A tangerine?

ZIETEK. Haven't you noticed? The city's flooded with 'em.

Everyone is taking tangerines.

PRUS. I haven't had a tangerine –

ZIETEK. You wait, we get the demonstrations up to half a million, it'll be bananas.

PRUS. Ah, but what about the General Strike?

ZIETEK. Ah. Pineapple.

MATKOVIC. Yes, what's always puzzled me, during the suppression, is who decided, what sub-committee, or who knows, what commission, sat down and *decided* that the way to punish us for Spassov and New Morning was to empty all the shops of everything but toilet roll and vinegar.

ZIETEK. Ah. Toilet roll.

PRUS (*with a paper*). Now everybody's clear, are they, that the first thing is that we insist -

ZIETEK. Hold on.

He puts on the ghetto-blaster. It's the American late 60s rock and roll.

MATKOVIC. Um, is this completely necessary?

PRUS *shrugs.* BRODSKAYA *is taking notes, but realises she's sticky.*

PRUS. Well, better safe than sorry. The first thing is that we insist, no assumptions and no preconditions. And the second is, we go on our agenda, and we go in order.

BRODSKAYA (*to* ZIETEK). Um, I don't suppose you've got a paper towel?

The main doors open. MONICA FREIE *enters with the trolley. She sees a group of counter-revolutionary plotters playing rock songs and eating tangerines.*

FREIE. Uh – oh.

PRUS. Why, Comrade Freie.

He switches off the ghetto-blaster.

FREIE. Um, I didn't think that you were meeting here.

PRUS. As yet, we're not. So, where d'you think –

FREIE. I'd understood, the August Victory Reception Room. Next door.

Slight pause.

They're obviously not ready for you yet.

She makes to go.

BRODSKAYA. D'you want a tangerine?

FREIE. Uh, no. No thanks.

ZIETEK. Go on.

FREIE. No, really. No.

PRUS. Um, Comrade.

FREIE. Yes?

PRUS. We have another member of our delegation. He's been delayed. Is it possible to show him to the August Victory Room? When he arrives?

FREIE. Oh, yes, I'm sure that's possible.

She makes to go.

ZIETEK. And, Comrade?

FREIE. Yes?

ZIETEK. What August victory?

She looks round the delegation, decides to say nothing, and goes out.

MATKOVIC. So he sent a message?

PRUS. No.

ZIETEK. A gift from God in my view.

MATKOVIC. What is?

ZIETEK. The delay.

PRUS. Shh. Shh. Or put the music on again.

KAPLAN, VLADISLAV *and* MILEV *come in through the small door.*

KAPLAN. Good afternoon. I'm so sorry. We've not met, I'm Kaplan.

He puts his hand out to PAVEL PRUS.

PRUS (*shaking*). How d'you do. I'm Prus.

KAPLAN. And this is Petr Vladislav, and this Jan Milev.

MATKOVIC. So this is just a party delegation?

KAPLAN. No, it's from the government. Mr Vladislav is the Minister of the Interior, and Mr Milev Minister of Labour, Health and Social Welfare. And I myself am the Prime Minister.

ZIETEK. And First Secretary of the Party.

KAPLAN. Temporarily, I trust.

PRUS. But there's no-one from the other parties in the Patriotic Bloc.

KAPLAN. Not for the present, no. These are after all preliminary talks. You'll note that your demand for an expansion of the bodies represented in the talks is high on our agenda.

ZIETEK. When you say 'agenda'?

KAPLAN. We have drawn up a preliminary agenda. Now, I think I recognise Professor Matkovic -

PRUS. I'm sorry. Jan Matkovic, Andrei Zietek, Victoria Brodskaya. Mr Zietek is a representative of the Free Workers Alliance, Professor Matkovic of the Forum of Church Councils and the editor of the unofficial journal Copyright, as I believe you are aware; and Miss Brodskaya is our secretary. All three are members of the Public Platform, of which I am through some oversight the President.

MILEV. You said 'Free Workers'.

PRUS. Yes.

MILEV. So what does Mr Zietek do?

PRUS. Mr Zietek is at present studying at the A.M.Gorky University.

MILEV. Aha.

PRUS. But Jan and I try and keep him up to date with working-class realities.

MILEV. I thought you said -

KAPLAN. I think Mr Prus refers to the fact that Professor Matkovic is a stoker in a foundry. And he himself cleans windows.

MILEV. Poor old him.

PRUS. Rather more thoroughly, if I may say so, than the person who cleans yours.

A tricky pause. VLADISLAV *wades in, his hand outstretched.*

VLADISLAV. How do you do. I'm very pleased to see you.

ZIETEK (*shaking hands*). Uh – hallo.

KAPLAN *follows, shaking hands with* ZIETEK.

KAPLAN. Mr Zietek, how d'you do.

Everyone shaking hands with everyone else.

PRUS. Mr Milev. I suppose I should say, congratulations on your new appointment.

MILEV. And on your release.

VLADISLAV (*with* MATKOVIC). I must say, that I've always got great pleasure from your editorials in Copyright.

KAPLAN (*to* BRODSKAYA). Hallo, I'm pleased to meet you.

VLADISLAV. I suspect indeed my Ministry has a more complete collection of back numbers than you do.

MATKOVIC. Well, it's entirely possible.

ZIETEK. Perhaps then Comrade Vladislav should give an interview.

VLADISLAV. Um, I –

ZIETEK. Though if you did of course you'd have then to arrest yourself. As an accessory to the dissemination of subversive propaganda.

VLADISLAV. Yes, I suppose I –

ZIETEK. But at least it's good to have a Minister of the Interior who can actually read. The last one, so they say, required fraternal help to tell the little boys' room from the little girls'.

Sticky pause.

KAPLAN. There's a similar, um, joke about L.Brezhnev. Apparently, when somebody knocked on his office door, he'd stand up, find a typed card, and read out 'come in'.

Most people laugh.

MILEV. Thought that was Ronald Reagan.

KAPLAN. Well, I suspect it's universally applicable. Now, in fact, we thought today we'd meet next door.

MATKOVIC. In the August Victory Reception Room.

KAPLAN. That's right. It's a little more informal.

Opposition looks at each other, as KAPLAN *begins to try to shepherd people to the door.*

And I think more comfortable, also, for a small group. We were in fact expecting five of you . . .

MATKOVIC. Yes, unfortunately, it seems -

PRUS. Prime Minister, just before we get too comfortable, there is one thing that I have to say.

KAPLAN. What's that?

PRUS. It's just to confirm we are all absolutely clear that there are no preconditions for these talks today.

Slight pause.

KAPLAN. What do you mean?

ZIETEK. He means we haven't said we'll call the strike off. Or the demonstrations.

KAPLAN. Is that −

PRUS. In a nutshell, yes.

Slight pause.

MILEV. So is there any point −

KAPLAN. I think . . . We hope of course that today's talks will result in a retreat from some entrenched positions. But the most important thing is that they happen. In Paris, the Americans and the

Vietnamese spent seven months agreeing the configuration of the delegations at the talks. Quite literally, the shape of the negotiating table. I think we can agree we haven't got that long.

Pause.

PRUS. Indeed. Which is why we've drawn up our own preliminary agenda.

Slight pause. The Government delegates look at each other.

Well, it's more what you might call, a reasonably uncontroversial statement of joint aims. That we felt we might agree on as a start.

Slight pause.

KAPLAN. Round one.

They go into the other room. On their way, MATKOVIC *finds himself with* VLADISLAV.

VLADISLAV. I might consider giving you an interview. Anything's frankly preferable to talking to the Star.

MATKOVIC. Ah, but with what preconditions?

VLADISLAV. Coffee?

They've gone. After a moment, enter FREIE. *She's about to clear the fizzy drinks on to her trolley. Then she has a thought. She goes to the phone and picks it up, and dials. Nothing. She puts it down, picks it up and listens. After a moment.*

FREIE. Hallo. Please, could I have a line?
Oh, right.
It's 21647.

Pause.

Oh. Oh, right.

She puts down the phone. She shrugs slightly, and goes to clear the fizzy drinks. Before doing so, she faces the moral dilemma of the tangerines. She overcomes this and begins to work. After a moment or two, VLADISLAV, KAPLAN *and* MILEV *hurry back in. They have carbon copies of a document.* FREIE *has no choice but to carry on with her task.*

MILEV. Uncontroversial. They said 'uncontroversial'?

VLADISLAV. Prime Minister, I'd suggest we go through this point by point -

MILEV. Comrade Prime Minister, I must protest –

VLADISLAV. – and at least establish what might be amended –

MILEV. – on behalf of all the working people of the Socialist
Republic –

KAPLAN. Comrades, please –

The phone rings. FREIE *wins the race with* VLADISLAV *to pick it up.*

FREIE. Hallo? Oh, yes.
Yes, yes it is.
No, actually, no. Not – now.

She puts the phone down.

It was, um – misdirected. Please excuse me.

She hurries out. A moment, then KAPLAN *reasserts the subject.*

KAPLAN. Now –

VLADISLAV. It's a negotiating position.

MILEV. It's a bloody ultimatum.

VLADISLAV. No it's not a bloody ultimatum. Ultimata are when you
say, unless you accept this as it is unchanged then such and such
will happen. No-one has said that. It is not an ultimatum.

MILEV. Oh well, I'm very sorry, of course I didn't go to University –

VLADISLAV. Oh, for God's sake.

KAPLAN. Please, comrades.

Pause.

We asked for a withdrawal so we could consider our response. To this
– this presentation. The other side appeared to understand that that
implied it is open to amendment.

KAPLAN *and* VLADISLAV *sit, to work on the document.*

MILEV. Oh, well, that's very good of them. I think we should
remember comrades who's the government of this country.

VLADISLAV. I think we should remember also what is happening out
there.

MILEV. And who's responsible for what is happening –

VLADISLAV. Which is that a quarter of a million people every day –

MILEV. And that if the present Minister of the Interior had listened to
the former First Secretary of the Party –

KAPLAN. Please. Now, Petr.

VLADISLAV *working on the document.*

VLADISLAV. 'Our country faces a profound political, economic and moral crisis. There is a need for radical and comprehensive change'.

KAPLAN. Well, we can all agree about the crisis.

MILEV. Oh, sure, there's a crisis.

KAPLAN. And the need for change.

MILEV. Yuh, I might suggest a few.

VLADISLAV (*amending*). So. 'Our country faces crisis. There is a need for change. Politically, there's an urgent need for the Constitution to be observed'. Shall we say, 'continue to be observed'?

MILEV. So it can't be urgent.

VLADISLAV. Right. 'And for non-governmental institutions to exist and operate effectively'. Once again, 'to continue to exist'. As, for example, the Trade Unions.

MILEV *shrugs.*

MILEV. OK.

VLADISLAV. 'Economically, the system of command has been found to be unwieldy and destructive. There is a need to open the economy to market forces and new forms of ownership'.

MILEV. What new forms?

KAPLAN. Yes, it's interesting they don't say 'opening to private capital'.

MILEV. How interesting?

KAPLAN. I mean that it implies cooperatives, workers' self-management . . .

VLADISLAV. Perhaps if we said, economically, the command system has on occasions tended to be ladida . . . to consider opening the economy . . .

KAPLAN. Or expanding. Adding rather than a substitution of new forms.

VLADISLAV. Indeed. 'Expanding's very good. 'While, morally, there is an urgent need' – again – 'for the restoration of accepted norms of public discourse, based on full freedom of information and full civil rights. A full investigation must be mounted into the party and the government's suppression of New Morning, the so-called consolidation, and all subsequent events'.

MILEV. Over my dead body.

KAPLAN. Well, they can't have thought they'd get away with that.

MILEV. Don't you believe it, comrade.

VLADISLAV. Well, we could cut the whole section. Go straight on to the final paragraph.

KAPLAN. Let's go on and come back to it.

VLADISLAV. 'Finally, while accepting the necessity of friendly relations with neighbouring countries, there is an overriding need for the creation of a fully independent sovereign national life, based on the principles of parliamentary democracy'.

MILEV. In other words, we junk the socialist fraternity of nations, and turn ourselves into a bourgeois state.

VLADISLAV. Whereas we could, while *not questioning* the existence of our international alliances, accept there is an overriding need for the *development* of a fully independent sovereign national life, on the principles of *socialist* democracy.

MILEV. The Minister is of the view they'll buy that? In a million years?

KAPLAN. If not, they don't get their joint statement.

Pause.

MILEV. Well, as long as you don't welsh on it -

KAPLAN. Comrade Milev, the word 'welsh' is really not appropriate to a conversation between colleagues in a government, or comrades in a party.

MILEV. Sorry.

He picks up the document.

Yes if we all agree to stick to it. Which we all have.

VLADISLAV. Um, we haven't done the fourth paragraph. The one that goes in over the Minister's dead body.

KAPLAN. Well, then, we'd better look at it.

VLADISLAV. Well, I would suggest in fact we cut it. After all, the substantive point is calling for investigation of the period of the consolidation, and that's already on the table.

MILEV. Is it?

VLADISLAV. Yes. It's in their New Dawn statement. Item nine.

MILEV. But we don't accept the New Dawn thing.

VLADISLAV. We accept it as a basis for negotiation.

MILEV. Oh, I see. Well doubtless if I was a university professor then I'd understand that.

VLADISLAV. Look. 'We all agree that Comrade Milev hasn't grasped the point'. Or 'We agree that while we don't agree yet on that question, we are willing to discuss the matter. And then subsequently come to a conclusion that commands the general agreement of both sides. As to whether Comrade Milev has or hasn't grasped the point'. Or is ever in a month of Sundays going to.

KAPLAN. Now, stop it, Petr. Jan knows full well what you mean.

VLADISLAV. Well, if so, he – I'm sorry.

Slight pause.

Or, I mean, I'm sorry.

Pause. KAPLAN *stands.*

KAPLAN. It is all subject to negotiation. It is a set of relatively small amendments. As they would expect. And I suggest we now present them to the opposition.

Pause.

MILEV. Right.

They go to the small door. KAPLAN *allows* MILEV *to go through.* KAPLAN *stops* VLADISLAV.

KAPLAN. That's not the way to do it.

VLADISLAV. No. I'm sorry.

KAPLAN. However, I wonder if there is a way to do it. In the final paragraph.

VLADISLAV. Do what?

KAPLAN. Kill three birds with one stone. Spassov, the leading role, the Warsaw Pact.

VLADISLAV. That's not a bird I think we ought to kill.

KAPLAN. Yes. Yes, I noticed that. No, I meant that if we did insist on sticking to our international obligations, a little modified perhaps, then we might amend the rest in such a way that might imply a softening on other matters. Not for now. To be kept in reserve.

VLADISLAV. Yes, well -

KAPLAN. You know, perhaps we shouldn't be too suspicious about what they mean by 'restoration'. After all, the word has its own meaning. As well as being code.

Re-enter MILEV.

MILEV. Excuse me. I thought we'd gone back in.

KAPLAN. I'm sorry. Yes, we're coming.

KAPLAN, VLADISLAV and MILEV go into the other room. After a moment, FREIE comes in again. Seeing the room is empty, she makes to begin to work. Then she sees the ghetto-blaster. She switches on the radio. It's British reggae. She carries on with her work. The record ends. The announcement is in German. She lets it run. A jingling German ad comes on. FREIE frowns, goes back to the radio, retunes. She goes through martial music with a stirring communist commentary, and hits gypsy music. She's about to retune again, when she notices the cassette. She puts it on, and then carries on working to the music. She finishes clearing the table. Perhaps she is even humming or singing along when ZIETEK, PRUS and MATKOVIC burst in, followed by BRODSKAYA.

ZIETEK. 'Amendments'. 'Relatively small amendments'.

PRUS. Now, perhaps we need to ask ourselves the question –

ZIETEK. There's only one question I can see worth asking –

PRUS. – what exactly our objectives are –

ZIETEK. Do we carry on with this charade –

PRUS. – and what can be achieved –

ZIETEK. – or do we bring the general strike forward –

MATKOVIC. Please can we have some quiet?

FREIE switches off the cassette.

PRUS. Miss Freie. I wonder if . . .

FREIE Yes. Yes. In fact, I've finished.

Gesturing to the cassette.

I'm very sorry, I –

PRUS. You're very welcome, really.

FREIE *goes out with her trolley.*

ZIETEK. You ought to have it on.

MATKOVIC. Well only if there's something other than the Rolling Stones.

ZIETEK. Jefferson Airplane. There is a radio.

PRUS. No, Andrei, leave it, please.

PRUS *sits, holds his head in his hands. Then he looks up. To* MATKOVIC:

So what d'you think?

MATKOVIC. I think . . . the thing we must remember . . . Is that the hardest thing in any battle is to notice when you've won.

ZIETEK. Pretty fucking difficult in this case.

PRUS. Be quiet, Andrei. Yes, go on.

MATKOVIC. Because when you've lost, it's easy. Your opponents let you know. Delighted to. But when you've won – they tend to keep it to themselves.

PRUS. All right. One. They've conceded there's a crisis and a need for change.

ZIETEK. Well, grudgingly.

MATKOVIC. So what did you expect? They run the country.

PRUS. But what they wouldn't budge on was specifics. So it was all tending and considering and expanding and continuing on the presently accepted course.

ZIETEK (*to* BRODSKAYA). This is a famous victory.

PRUS. And, while they're not too bothered about reassessing the suppression, all that stuff that sticks to Lutz, they are quite jumpy about things more recently.

ZIETEK. Surprise, surprise.

PRUS. And they clearly won't budge on infringement of our national sovereignty. So, if instead of what they've given us, our para five, whereas, whereas . . . there is an overriding need for the, what was it?

ZIETEK. Oh, for heaven's sake.

BRODSKAYA *hands him the paper.*

BRODSKAYA. 'Development'.

PRUS. Development.

ZIETEK. It's only words.

PRUS. Not 'only', Andrei.

MATKOVIC. Isn't that what we're discussing?

ZIETEK. Oh, sure. And when the SDU has smashed the demonstrations, and the DNS has shoved us all in jail, and we've really lost, then perhaps Professor Matkovic might deign to notice it?

PRUS. Now, stop it, Andrei.

ZIETEK. 'Cos it's just the same as poor old Spassov. It's the idea that if you get the words right, if you get them to accept a 'negative development' or a 'threat to socialist normality' instead of 'counter-revolution', then it doesn't matter that your government's been kidnapped and a foreign army's in your streets. And if I was you, Pavel, and Victor Spassov turned up in this room, and started whingeing on about how after all in the context of the balance of political formations at the time he did his best but he was up against these 'fundamental geopolitical realities', I'd tell him that his forms of words put you and thousands more like you in jail.

PRUS, *angry, bangs on the cassette.*

PRUS. OK. Now Andrei, let's just get this business straight -

KAPLAN, VLADISLAV *and* MILEV *have re-entered through the small door.*

KAPLAN. Is this a party?

PRUS *switches off the cassette player.*

I'm sorry. We took the opportunity to take another look at our proposed amendments to your document. You might like to take a glance at it.

VLADISLAV *tries to hand the document to* PRUS *but* ZIETEK *is nearer and gets it first.*

VLADISLAV (*handing over a document to* PRUS). I'm sorry about the handwriting.

KAPLAN. Lenin is reputed to have signed the order for the Russian

Revolution with a stub of pencil on a scrap of children's graph
paper.

ZIETEK. Looks just the same.

KAPLAN. The changes are quite minor, certainly. Please, take your
time.

*KAPLAN, MILEV and VLADISLAV go out. MATKOVIC takes the
document from ZIETEK.*

PRUS. So, what –

ZIETEK. Pavel, it is identical. It's just the fucking same.

MATKOVIC. Victoria. Could you please ask the Prime Minister to
come back in. On a tiny point of clarification.

BRODSKAYA. Yes of course.

MATKOVIC. If possible, just him.

BRODSKAYA goes out.

ZIETEK. What's going on?

PRUS. What is it Jan?

MATKOVIC. Oh, it's nothing, probably. Just the form of words. It's
just, it isn't quite the fucking same.

*Re-enter BRODSKAYA, with KAPLAN, MILEV and VLADISLAV. She
gives a little shrug, to indicate she tried to keep it just KAPLAN, but all three
came.*

KAPLAN. Professor Matkovic.

MATKOVIC. Prime Minister. When in this revision you say that we
shouldn't question the existence of our present international treaty
obligations . . .

KAPLAN. Yes?

MATKOVIC. . . . as opposed that is to our 'alliances', would it imply, I
wonder, a somewhat narrower interpretation of our responsibilities
to those states with which were currently aligned?

Slight pause.

KAPLAN. Well, it might be possible to draw such a conclusion, yes.

MATKOVIC. And the fact that the development of a full independent
sovereign national life is now 'the restoration of a fully independent
so and so forth . . .' that would indicate that we were once sovereign

and then lost that sovereignty?

Slight pause.

KAPLAN. Yes, that certainly might be implied.

MATKOVIC. Perhaps in the period we were in receipt of fraternal international assistance?

Pause.

KAPLAN. Well you could put that interpretation on it, clearly.

MILEV. Comrade –

MATKOVIC. And last, I note, the 'principles of socialist democracy' are now 'the principles of socialism and democracy'.

KAPLAN. Are they?

He takes the document and looks at it.

So they are.

He hands back the document. He glances at VLADISLAV. *It's clear he's not going to volunteer anything else.*

MATKOVIC. With the implication that the two are not in all ways necessarily identical.

Pause. KAPLAN *is not going to help* VLADISLAV *here.*

VLADISLAV. Well, that would appear to follow, yes.

MATKOVIC. So it would be at least theoretically possible to have socialism without democracy –

VLADISLAV. Unlikely, but conceivable . . .

MATKOVIC. Or indeed the other way round.

Now VLADISLAV *won't go any further.*

VLADISLAV. No. No, I'm sure we would insist they're mutually dependent. Just not – identical.

MATKOVIC. The party's leading role?

KAPLAN. The party as – the leading partner.

MILEV *turns to* KAPLAN. *But* PRUS *quickly interrupts.*

MILEV. Comrade, I'm sure -

PRUS. Prime Minister, I think from our side we have the basis to recommend proceeding to full talks.

KAPLAN. With all that that implies?

PRUS. Insofar as what is happening out there is under our control.

ZIETEK. And subject to approval by our general body.

VLADISLAV. Naturally. And ours.

MATKOVIC. And our agreeing on the constitution of the talks.

MILEV. The constitution?

PRUS. Who's invited. Who sits where.

KAPLAN. Oh, you know, I really don't think that will prove a problem. For, Mr Prus, I think we're entering, or we have entered, now, your magic land where everything is possible, and things aren't always what they seem.

He pulls the tablecloth off the great table. It is revealed to be a number of smaller tables, of modern manufacture, set together to form the big rectangle. He pulls the end of one of the smaller tables away from the others, to demonstrate the geometric possibilities.

I'd say, there's room for everyone.

A man in his early 60s stands in the doorway.

SPASSOV. Excuse me. I'm so sorry, I have been delayed.

They all look at him.

My train was stopped three times, and searched by customs officers. Most odd. It's not an international train.

People are looking at him as if he's a ghost.

I'm the bourgeois restorationist V. Spassov. Have I come to the right room?

Blackout.
End of Act One.

ACT TWO

Scene One

The room is now set out for a full meeting. Covered in crisp white cloths, the tables have been formed into three sides of a big square. (In the centre is a floral arrangement). Glasses, bottles, openers and ashtrays on the table. In the room, waiting for the meeting to start, are PRUS, ZIETEK., MATKOVIC, BRODSKAYA, SPASSOV and ROUSOVA. BRODSKAYA and PRUS are assembling piles of documents for the meeting. There are also other delegates, including a BISHOP, a SOCIAL DEMOCRAT, and a severe YOUNG WOMAN. The atmosphere is quite tense, and there is a quiet buzz of conversation. It dies when LUTZ walks into the room through the main doors.

LUTZ. I'm sorry. Am I late?

Everyone is looking at him.

My name's Lutz. I'm the Chairman of the General Federation of Trade Unions. I understood there was a meeting to which we'd been invited.

Slight pause.

Well, if it isn't Victor Spassov. Glory be.

SPASSOV. Josef. I thought they'd sacked you.

LUTZ. Just demoted. Like you and that Cultural Attachéship we put you in in Brazzaville.

SPASSOV. Nairobi.

LUTZ. From which we all assumed that you'd defect.

SPASSOV. In a time of crisis one does not desert one's country.

LUTZ. Quite agree.

He looks round the room.

Well, then. New Government. Hardliners routed. The Principles of Democratic Pluralism finally triumphant. All those previous dogmatic shortcomings and errors rectified. I guess you'll all be feeling pretty bloody smug.

In fact, no-one looks very smug, but before anyone can react, KAPLAN, VLADISLAV, MILEV, FREIE *and the uniformed* MINISTER OF DEFENCE *enter through the small door. This group is cheerful, and* KAPLAN *in particular is highly energised and confident. He moves quickly and efficiently round the other* NEGOTIATORS.

KAPLAN. Good morning.

PRUS. Morning.

VLADISLAV. Morning.

After KAPLAN *shakes hands with* NEGOTIATORS, *they get to their places.*

KAPLAN. Mr Prus. And Victor.

SPASSOV. Michal.

VLADISLAV. Madame Rousova. Hallo. And – Bishop . . .

KAPLAN. Comrade Kapekovna. Mr . . .

LUTZ. Hallo, Petr.

VLADISLAV. Comrade.

KAPLAN. Josef. How are you? So, shall we make a start?

He sits, along with MILEV, VLADISLAV, FREIE *and the* MINISTER OF DEFENCE *on the central side of the arrangement of tables. On one of the two arms are the* PUBLIC PLATFORM *delegation, including* SPASSOV; *opposite them are* BRODSKAYA, LUTZ, *the* BISHOP, *the* SOCIAL DEMOCRAT *and the* YOUNG WOMAN. *When all are settled,* KAPLAN *begins his introduction.*

KAPLAN. Comrades and friends. Resulting from informal talks, this is the first full dialogue between the government and the widest range of representatives, drawn from all sectors of our national life. We hope this meeting – taking place under the most optimistic circumstances, as I'm sure you'll all agree – will prove the first of many.

He expects a more positive reaction. He doesn't get it, so ploughs on.

We have a Bishop, a professor – and as it happens no less than three delegates who are now or have been First Secretary of the Communist Party. This must I think constitute some sort of record.

There is not very much response to this joke either. KAPLAN *is beginning to pick up the tension in the room.*

And representatives of the National Peasants' party, the Social Democratic Party and the League of Youth. Once again I gather Miss –

He checks a note.

– Brodskaya will be taking notes for the Public Platform – side, and today we welcome Comrade Freie to perform the same task for the Government. I should of course say the new Government, of National Understanding.

By now he realises this will not get the expected response. So he finishes off on a firmer tack.

Whose formation is the consequence of the welcome easing of the social tensions which have so afflicted us in recent days. Whose members are drawn from the broadest social spheres, many represented here today. Which has already taken action on some urgent and important matters.

He wants some help. Slight pause.

ROUSOVA Perhaps, Prime Minister, we might know what they are.

KAPLAN. Yes. Petr.

VLADISLAV *reads out a statement.*

VLADISLAV. One. The Government of National Understanding will put to the National Assembly new laws to amend the legal code on education. From now on, the requirement on the schools to teach the precepts and philosophy of Marxist-Leninism will be ended, and replaced with more general principles of scientific knowledge and humanitarianism.
Two. The Commission of Investigation into the period of the Consolidation will begin its hearings, openly, in public, from next Tuesday.
Three. In acknowledgement of certain drawbacks and inflexibilities in the national economy, the number of persons that can be employed by private individuals or cooperative endeavours will be increased from five to 300.

LUTZ. What?

VLADISLAV. And, in order to secure much needed capital investment, foreign companies will henceforward be permitted to take a non-controlling stake in national enterprises.

LUTZ *looks fixedly at* MILEV, *who indicates this wasn't his idea.*

Oh, and four, on a matter which appears to be of public interest, the red star will be taken off the national flag.

KAPLAN. This is basically a safety measure. It appears to be so difficult to burn the star out without a major conflagration.

Slight pause.

I should say that there was some pressure for the old imperial crest to be restored. Which we felt inappropriate. For a modern country in our modern age.

VLADISLAV. Also, reverting to the old words of the national Anthem does not appear to us a great priority.

KAPLAN. So, are there any questions?

SPASSOV. Yes. May I ask, who is on the Commission of Investigation?

KAPLAN. It is not yet finally determined.

ZIETEK. So who's chairing it?

KAPLAN. As you would expect, for a Commission on such a matter, the new Minister of Justice. Not a member of our party, and a schoolgirl at the time. So, can we generally conclude –

PRUS. Prime Minister.

KAPLAN. Yes Mr Prus.

PRUS. You know as well as I do that all these announcements are most welcome.

KAPLAN. I'm most pleased to hear it.

PRUS. As you also know that they are quite inadequate as a response to the demands that Public Platform have put to the Government.

Pause.

KAPLAN. Go on.

PRUS *is shuffling a lot of papers.*

PRUS. We too I think have four points. First. Of course we welcome any liberalisation of the economy. But we still doubt whether this is meaningful, while the governmental party still has exclusive access to the workplace.

KAPLAN. You mean –

MILEV. They mean factory branches of the Party.

PRUS. Right. We've brought this up before, of course. In fact, we've drawn up some proposals for the legal changes we believe are indispensible to end the Communist monopoly of public life.

He hands round the first of several piles of documents.

You needn't read it now.

MILEV. Well, thanks.

PRUS. Second. I have to tell you Public Platform considers that 'restoration of full national sovereignty' relies on rapid extradition – sorry, that must be, extrication? – of our forces from those of the Warsaw Pact, and the evacuation of all foreign forces from our soil. We have in fact drawn up a timetable for this as well.

A second pile of papers is handed round.

I'm sure there's something less, well, anal than 'evacuation'.

He watches the papers go round for a moment.

While, third, we do insist that any investigation of the last 20 years covers the last 20 years, and not just what the government insists on calling the 'period of the consolidation', following 'receipt of international fraternal help'. Which we, we think more accurately, call 'the period of the suppression after the invasion'. Vicky, please.

BRODSKAYA *hands round copies of a further document.*

PRUS. This is a list of areas, and indeed specific incidents, of illegal and repressive actions by the party and the government, which we feel demand the fullest possible investigation by the Minister of Justice, whoever she or he may be.

Government eyebrows are raised, both at the list and the implication that the Minister of Justice might change.

Of course we may have left some out. After all, there are so many.

KAPLAN. Yes, I see.

Slight pause.

VLADISLAV. Um, when you say, 'whoever' –

PRUS. Fourth –

MILEV. There's more?

PRUS. Four items, yes. Like yours.

He shuffles papers.

In fact, you are the item.

He looks at the Government delegation. Then he reads from a hastily assembled set of papers.

The following was endorsed by a plenary assembly of the Public Platform, in the small hours of today. 'This meeting notes the formation of the so-called Government of Nationa! Understanding. The composition of this government, 12 Communists, six members of the coalition parties of the Patriotic Bloc, and five so-called independent experts, in reality no more than window-dressing for what is still a party-dominated administration. It views this government as totally inadequate as a response to the events of recent days. It points out that by no means everybody in the government is untainted by events of the 18th'. November, obviously. 'It regards it as an insult both to the injured of the 18th and to all those persecuted under so-called socialism in this country. It refuses to accept this government, and insists instead that a true Government of National Renewal be installed, taking it as axiomatic that such a government will have a majority of Ministers who are not members of the present ruling party'.

BRODSKAYA *points to a correction.*

PRUS. Ah. That's an 'absolute majority'.

He looks up.

I'm sorry. It's a bit repetitive. And there's a sentence with no verb. But it was put together at some speed.

MATKOVIC. And very late at night.

ZIETEK. By upwards of two hundred very angry people.

PRUS. There are no copies I'm afraid.

Pause.

KAPLAN. When you say 'under so-called socialism' . . .

ZIETEK. Oh, it means just 'under socialism'.

SPASSOV *looks to* PRUS.

PRUS. Too many 'so-calleds' anyway.

Pause.

VLADISLAV. I have, I have two questions.

KAPLAN *waves him on.*

The first is whether the opposition is aware than the government has not ruled out further widening of the government. And if, in their, um, their 'minor reconstruction of the Government', if the opposition groupings would insist on any, on particular formations being represented. Like, themselves.

PRUS. Well, I can't speak for other groupings. But equally I can't think that a person seriously considering a government for this Republic, now, would not consider, say, Professor Matkovic.

VLADISLAV. Yes. I see. My second question is a point from earlier. It is, if Mr Prus – considers, that the so-called 'timetable' for military withdrawal of our allies from our soil accords with the last statement that he put his name to on this subject. In which he may recall he accepted the existence and presumably the content of our present international treaty obligations.

PRUS *looks to* MATKOVIC.

MATKOVIC. Yes, I think we'd say it's a development of that.

VLADISLAV. 'Development'?

MATKOVIC. A development and a revision.

VLADISLAV. In other words, what's happening is that you are reneging on agreements of three days ago.

MILEV. Or welshing, even.

MATKOVIC. No, I think we are acknowledging what's happening now.

PRUS. Or indeed what could well happen, if we didn't reach agreement here today.

ZIETEK. By way of tightening of tensions previously eased. Out there.

Pause. KAPLAN *stands.*

KAPLAN. That is a threat.

MILEV. If not an ultimatum.

KAPLAN. To the legitimate and legal Government of the Republic.

ZIETEK. Oh. Legitimate.

KAPLAN. And I must ask you to withdraw it.

There is silence.

We have. We have moved a great deal further, we have done much more, than you, or anyone, had any right . . . But of course how you respond is up to you.

He doesn't know what to do.

LUTZ. Comrade Prime Minister. A point of order.

KAPLAN. Yes?

LUTZ. These are matters vital to the future of our country. We have heard a lot from Public Platform on these matters. I wonder if you planned to hear the views of anybody else.

Slight pause.

Seeing as how we've all turned up.

At least this will stop KAPLAN *having to walk out. So he sits.*

KAPLAN. Please, please.

LUTZ. I don't know for example if Madame Rousova might care to speculate as to the likely general view among the National Peasantry about the government's proposals for the restitution of the landlord class . . .

ROUSOVA. Would that there were.

LUTZ. Or if Professor Matkovic might care to venture an opinion on the likely nature of the, what?

He checks a note.

– the 'scientific and humanitarian principles' on which our education system is now to be based. An education system which, ironically, can claim some credit for producing Messrs Prus and Zietek. If not actually himself.

MATKOVIC *decides not to respond.*

While I myself might have some comments on the rights of people to organise politically at their place of work. And about reneging on our promise to the working class to end the crime of capital accumulation and the exploitation of one man by another.

To MATKOVIC:

I mean, just tell me, when you smuggle out your tasteful little essays for the fashionable Western quarterlies to publish under clever pseudonyms, when you pour your lordly and patrician scorn on the debased plebeian culture of the upstart proletarians who have seized

your country from your kind, how do you look at them? Your fellow
workers? In your foundry? In the morning? Do they know the things
you say about them? Would it matter? Would you care?

MATKOVIC *says nothing. Pause.*

KAPLAN. Comrade. The points you make are points on all our minds.
But I suspect that we have moved beyond the point where anything is
served by making them.

Pause.

We will withdraw for I hope no longer than five minutes. Please.

KAPLAN, VLADISLAV, MILEV, FREIE *and the* MINISTER OF
DEFENCE *go out.*

SPASSOV (*to* PRUS). Well -

LUTZ. So, Victor. Your 'new morning'. Smiling socialism. The saviour,
or the gravedigger? I'm sorry. You'll be wanting to draw up your new
demands.

ZIETEK *snaps his fingers and stands.*

ZIETEK. The Ministries.

PRUS. I'm sorry?

ZIETEK. We forgot to say the Ministries.

He's heading for the small door when MILEV *comes through it.*

MATKOVIC. Well, that was quick.

MILEV (*to* ZIETEK, *who is inadvertently blocking his way*). Excuse me
please.

He goes to LUTZ *and whispers to him, gesturing at some of the Public
Platform papers. He goes back to the door.* LUTZ – *leaving his cigarettes and
matches and perhaps some papers on the table – stands and follows. At the
door he turns back. To* SPASSOV, *wickedly:*

LUTZ. Write me a letter.

He goes out. MILEV *aware of* ZIETEK.

MILEV. Uh – Can I help you?

ZIETEK. Yes. There's something we forgot.

MILEV. What's that?

ZIETEK. We want three Ministries.

MILEV. Just three?

ZIETEK. No, three specifically.

MILEV. Go on.

ZIETEK. Communications, Justice, the Interior.

Slight pause.

MILEV. You're joking. You're not serious.

ZIETEK. We're absolutely serious.

Slight pause.

MILEV. Right then. I'll pass it on.

He goes out.

SPASSOV. They'll never give you that.

ZIETEK. They never 'gave' us anything. That's the mistake we keep on making. That's the mistake you made.

ZIETEK *returns to the table.*

MATKOVIC. Nonetheless, it would surely be good to hear Victor's opinion of the course we should pursue. In the event of what we must presume will be the government's response.

PRUS. Well, yes.

MATKOVIC. Which will no doubt be drawn from straight rejection, or prevarication, or delay.

ZIETEK. Or they say yes.

PRUS. In which case, it would prove we've set our sights too low, and we'll be strung up by a vengeful populace. So, then –

ZIETEK. And we have this conversation here and now?

He's referring to the other people in the room.

PRUS. Why not. We don't have anything to hide. It's not us who have governed from behind locked doors for 40 years.

Slight pause.

So, anyone is welcome to contribute. Really. Please.

Pause.

SPASSOV. In my opinion, I would say there are three crucial features of the situation we should note. The first is that in the new government there are no ministers associated with the hard-line faction in the party. No Skuratov, no Gero. And the second is that Vladislav held out a further widening of the government. And the third is that Kaplan was genuinely surprised by your response. I'd say that was significant, at least.

MATKOVIC. I suppose the question is, if we believe them. On the further widening.

PRUS. Or if Kaplan can deliver.

ZIETEK. Or if he's been set up.

MATKOVIC. 'Set up'?

ZIETEK. By Lutz and Milev. Why was Lutz called back?

PRUS. Custer's last stand.

MATKOVIC. Or else to say, look at these people. You give them what they want, they spit it back at you.

PRUS. You could say, he had cause to think we'd buy it. 'Leading Partner'.

MATKOVIC. The question is, do we need Kaplan still in place.

PRUS. We do if the alternative is Lutz.

SPASSOV. But in reality of course the alternative is Vladislav.

  ZIETEK, PRUS *and* MATKOVIC *look at each other.*

  Surely Vladislav is preferable to either Lutz or Kaplan.

PRUS. Well, he might be. But I'm afraid he's really not an option.

ZIETEK. You're afraid?

  PRUS *gestures at the piles of paper.*

PRUS. The point of all the paper was the list. The list of incidents to be investigated.

  Other people still look confused.

  Which will, um – do, for Josef Lutz. But will also do for Petr Vladislav.

  Slight pause.

MATKOVIC. So it's Kaplan or it's going back.

ZIETEK. Or going forward.

He stands and marches to the window.

I mean, we're talking as if we can turn this on and off like a tap. We talk as if the point of this is to save those bastards' skins. Whereas out there, they don't want Vladislav or Kaplan. They want something else.

ROUSOVA. Yes, it's interesting to speculate, exactly what that 'something' is.

Pause.

MATKOVIC. Madame Rousova?

ROUSOVA. Because although I yield to no-one in my view of the importance of the flag, and the reassertion of our national heritage and character, and consigning Comrade Lutz and his associates to history's dustbin, really the most important thing to be said today was said very early on.

PRUS. And what was that?

ROUSOVA. That foreign companies will henceforward be permitted to take a stake in national enterprises.

MATKOVIC. They said a non-controlling stake.

ROUSOVA. Come, come, Professor. That is what they're saying now.

She stands and goes to the window, to ZIETEK's *discomfort.*

You see, I wonder if 'out there' they've really grasped what's going on. If they realise that they're exchanging the Red Flag for the pop song. Pravda for Playboy. The hammer and the sickle for the strip-joint, cola tin and burger-bar. To have expelled the Germans and the Russians just to hand the whole thing over to – America.

Slight pause.

I sometimes think we are the only Europeans left. We in the so-called Camp of Peace and Socialism. Since the West became a New York colony.

Pause. SPASSOV *stands.*

SPASSOV. There is some truth in that.

Slight pause. Moving a little away.

Notwithstanding that there have been contradictions –

ZIETEK. Oh, for Christ's sake.

ZIETEK *strides back to his side of the table.*

PRUS. Andrei.

ZIETEK. 'Contradictions'. Christ.

SPASSOV. I'm sorry?

ZIETEK. I just think we should remember something. If we're carving up the future of this country.

MATKOVIC. No-one's carving up this country.

ZIETEK (*to* PRUS). I think we should remember that there have been, since the end of the reform, a, what, a dozen major statements and petitions? On the Human Rights Day, the Warsaw Pact, the suppression of the bands, Helsinki? Friendship Park? None signed by her, none signed by him, all signed by you. I think we should remember.

Pause. With a slight smile, ROUSOVA *returns to her seat.*

PRUS. I didn't sign the Scrap the Pact thing. I thought it was mistimed.

ZIETEK. Well, what a sell-out. Cowardly old you. While the former First Secretary was really standing up for justice, freedom and democracy. Swanning round as Cultural Attaché in wherever.

PRUS. That is not fair. Mr Spassov was recalled. And has since then been a filing clerk. In a provincial office of the Ministry of Fuel.

SPASSOV *returns to his seat and sits.*

Now I would suggest that we secure at least a definite commitment to a realistic timetable. Vicky, please –

BRODSKAYA (*to* SPASSOV). So aren't you going to reply?

Slight pause.

SPASSOV. I'm sorry?

BRODSKAYA. This man has just accused you of, what, cowardice? Collaboration? Treachery? And you just sit there saying nothing.

SPASSOV. Well, naturally, I, uh –

BRODSKAYA. And all of you. They say the most extraordinary, outrageous things. And you just sit there talking about deals and timetables. Or the terrors of fast food and Coca-Cola. 'Vicky, please'.

Pause.

PRUS. Um -

BRODSKAYA (*to* SPASSOV). Don't get me wrong. I understand you
did your best and that there were realities and problems that we
don't have now. But I was born six days before they chucked you out.
I was supposed to be a child of the new morning. That's why my
parents called me by your name. That's why I'm called Victoria.

Pause.

SPASSOV. So then. What would you say?

BRODSKAYA. What would I say?

SPASSOV. They walk back in. And try to fix a deal. Or start
prevaricating. One of the Professor's options. So. What would you
say?

Slight pause.

BRODSKAYA. I'd ask them why they are prepared to lose factories but
not the party branches. Why they'll give up education but they won't
let go the police. I'd ask why the fact of power seems to be so much,
much more important than the things you do with it. And I'd ask
them how they feel about 'a so-called socialist society' which
promises a new Jerusalem but offers tangerines. In which the rule is,
if you want to eat, then keep you mouth shut. Which pledges the
collective liberation of all humankind but actually makes people
greedy, selfish, cynical and sly. In which no-one actually feels
responsible to anyone or anything beyond themselves. And who they
hell they think we are. And what they take us for.

She sees that KAPLAN, MILEV, LUTZ, FREIE *and the* MINISTER OF
DEFENCE *have re-entered. They look at her.*

I'm sorry. I am just the secretary.

She sits. Pause.

LUTZ. There is nothing wrong with being just the secretary. They are
people who can have great influence, upon the course of things.
Stalin was just the secretary.

*He walks to his place at the table, picks up his cigarettes and remaining
papers.*

But in answer to your question. One of them at least. You should ask
Comrade Vladislav to whom he is responsible. I think the answer will
be most illuminating.

He looks round the table.

I was once in fact just the secretary myself.

He goes out by the main doors. KAPLAN *sits, followed by the rest of the Government* DELEGATION.

KAPLAN. I'm sorry. This took a little longer than expected. So.

He reads from a paper.

The Government. The Government accepts the disbandment of all party branches in the workplaces, and will present legislation to the National Assembly to, to that effect.

New page.

The Government endorses the proposal of the Public Platform for the full investigation of the actions taken by the present leaders of the country in the period of so-called reform, the period of the consolidation, and in all years following.

New page.

The Government will not agree however to renege on international agreements with regard to military alliances and the stationing of troops. As you would expect. From the Government as constituted presently.

Pause. New page.

While, finally . . . Within three days, the Prime Minister will put to the President a further list of Ministers, drawn from an even wider spectrum of society. And in which no one particular – political formation will predominate.

He looks up.

I should say that I will not be putting my own name forward as Prime Minister. I should also say, that I have telephoned the President, who tells me that when he has fulfilled his duties in this matter, he too will resign.

MATKOVIC. And be replaced?

KAPLAN. Well, yes, eventually of course.

MATKOVIC. And how will the new President be chosen?

KAPLAN. Oh, I'd think, in any way that the new government decides.

PRUS. In other words -

KAPLAN. In other words, it's up to you.

Pause. The PUBLIC PLATFORM *delegation looks at each other. It sinks in.* ZIETEK *takes his ghetto-blaster from under the table and plonks it on the table.* KAPLAN *stands.*

So if there's nothing else –

ZIETEK *starts the machine. On the tape is a rather tinny instrumental. It is the National Anthem.* ZIETEK *begins to sing the words, and stands.* OTHERS *gradually join in and stand too, including the rest of the Government.*

THE ANTHEM. In our hearts, now and forever,
　　Dwells this land on which we gaze;
　　Ties that shall not split or sever
　　Bind us to its endless praise:
　　Loyal e'er and faithless never,
　　Thus we thy proud standard raise.

In the second verse, we hear the odd word sung differently by ZIETEK *and* MATKOVIC; *the rest of the* PUBLIC PLATFORM *delegation,* ROUSOVA *and the* BISHOP *getting the point and joining in. The* GOVERNMENT, SPASSOV *and others stick with what is in fact the New Version of the Anthem, as opposed to the Old Version the* OPPOSITION *is insisting on.*

THE ANTHEM. Black oppression justly spawning

OLD VERSION. Final national
NEW VERSION. Socialism's

THE ANTHEM. victory;
　　Dark the night but bright the dawning
　　Of a

OLD VERSION. nation
NEW VERSION. people

THE ANTHEM. yoked-now-free;
　　Across the land breaks our new morning,

OLD VERSION. Crowned with wreaths of majesty.
NEW VERSION. Forged in fires of history.

The last verse was very substantially changed when the Communists took over. Those who are singing the new version peter out well before the end.

NEW VERSION Freed from bloody subjugation
　　Tempered for a ceaseless fight,
　　Towards the final liberation,
　　To the endless future bright;

Spurning lies . . .

It has petered out by now.
Sung against:

OLD VERSION. Washed in blood of generations,
    Purified by ceaseless toil,
    Pledge we to the preservation
    Of our holy, ancient soil:
    To hand on blood and soil and nation
    To our children unbespoiled.

At the end of the anthem, there is a moment of silence. Suddenly rock music
breaks in on the tape, at the point where ZIETEK's recording of the anthem
finished. This breaks the tension, and, as ZIETEK switches the tape off, there
is much back-slapping and handshaking within the OPPOSITION, and
then between the OPPOSITION and the GOVERNMENT. Then the
various DELEGATIONS disperse, leaving SPASSOV, KAPLAN and
MILEV behind.

MILEV (*to* SPASSOV). Well, Comrade. I imagine you feel satisfied.

SPASSOV. Well, yes, I consider the outcome of the meeting –

MILEV. Vindicated, even.

SPASSOV. Certainly –

MILEV. I was brought up in the heart of district seven. On the fifth
    floor of a tenement that won the District Party Star for membership
    recruitment eight years running. From 1955 to 1962. But there was
    this one old biddy who just wouldn't budge. She stuck to Father Son
    and Holy Ghost through thick and thin. And when she was asked
    why, she'd say: Because I'll never open up the paper in the morning
    and see 'God Found Dead – Official'.

So what will they read tomorrow in the paper? The other people in
    the block? The ones with all those faded party stars? Now they're old
    too?

Pause.

I'm glad that you feel vindicated, comrade.

MILEV *goes out. Pause.*

KAPLAN. As so you should.

He pours himself a fizzy drink.

SPASSOV. I still – I don't see why.

KAPLAN. Why what?

SPASSOV. Why you needed to resign. Why you couldn't have led the process of reform. Why you couldn't have aligned –

KAPLAN. Yes, it is odd. The moment it becomes – untenable. It's like, in those American cartoons, when a character runs off a cliff, but keeps on going, running in mid air, till he looks down. And sometimes, I'd imagine, you don't quite spot the moment, when you realise there's actually nothing underneath your feet at all.

Slight pause.

But this case, it was very clear. It was when we understood the full – enormity of Mr Prus' little list of party infamies. Which could well put Josef Lutz in jail. Which will certainly destroy whatever moral standing our great party still has in the tenements of district seven. And which will also as it happens put paid to the reputation of one Petr Vladislav.

SPASSOV. What, Vladislav's corrupt?

KAPLAN. Well, he had a country cottage and a car. But no Swiss bank accounts or unofficial jaunts abroad. No, Petr's problem is of all things a pop concert in the park. Last spring, when he was Deputy Minister of the Interior. And he thought he'd done a deal, with the organisers, that they'd keep it within bounds, and he'd let it go ahead. Sadly for him, some hooligan leaps up and sings a song inciting people to refuse their military service, and the SDU goes in to break it up. Which it does with customary vigilance. But it's never been quite clear who gave the actual order. But I can't see it staying unclear for too long.

SPASSOV. I see.

KAPLAN. He was quite furious. He felt he'd been betrayed, you see. Which under the circumstances of today – is a very bitter irony.

Pause.

That's when you ask me what I mean.

SPASSOV (*not following*). What do you mean?

KAPLAN. I mean that it has now emerged, as I should have realised but didn't, that Petr Vladislav has from then till now been acting for the Russians. That the script for all this was written in Dzherzinsky Square. That according to that script, which is performed of course with Petr's usual zeal and dedication, Lutz and the hardliners are manoeuvred out of office, the economy is liberalised, the basis for a kind of market system's laid, but we're to hang on like grim death to ultimate political and military control. Which all works very nicely, till you dredge up Friendship Park, and Petr is one might say overtaken by his own event.

Slight pause.

SPASSOV. But surely, he believed in it –

KAPLAN. Well, Judas I've no doubt *believed* in it.

SPASSOV. Judas?

KAPLAN. Yes, I'm sorry, that's grotesque. Shall we just say, that if one's being played upon, it's nice to know about it. Even if one likes the tune.

Slight pause.

Which is why I had had some sympathy for his predicament, last spring. But now I think he had it coming. Actually.

Pause.

SPASSOV. Why tell all this to me?

KAPLAN. Oh, glasnost?

Slight pause.

I just thought you'd like the irony. That this revolution was set in train by the very people who put paid to yours. As Marx perceptively reminds us, the events of history occuring twice. First time as tragedy, the second time as farce.

SPASSOV. So that's – why it became untenable.

KAPLAN. Shall we say, it forced us to look down.

Pause. KAPLAN *goes to the window.*

Or rather, to look out. Out there. Through all the grime and dirty smears across the glass. To where the real history is happening.

Pause. He turns back to SPASSOV.

So, are you going to run?

SPASSOV. What do you mean?

KAPLAN. For office. It's a novel concept, I agree.

SPASSOV. Which office did you have in mind?

KAPLAN. The Presidency of the country. It's largely ceremonial of course, at present, but that too could change.

Slight pause.

SPASSOV. It hadn't crossed my mind.

KAPLAN. Come come.

SPASSOV. But it has now.

KAPLAN. That's better.

Making to go, he turns back:

Take a tip. I'll bet that Public Platform goes for getting Prus or somebody appointed by the National Assembly. Insist instead they hold a general, direct election, soon. They're not so popular outside the capital. All that stuff about effete self-advertisers cuts more ice out there. As well of course as being absolutely true.

SPASSOV *takes a moment to assess this.*

SPASSOV. And what about yourself?

KAPLAN. What me? Oh, no. I think I have my place in history.

SPASSOV *looks questioningly at* KAPLAN.

I am the last ambassador. I am standing on the roof, and waiting for the final helicopter, with the red flag folded underneath my arm.

Enter VLADISLAV *through the small door.* SPASSOV *and* KAPLAN *turn to him.*

VLADISLAV. The Ministry of Information has announced the changes in the Government.

To be flashed around the world in seconds. Via telex, modem, fibre optic cable. Satellite, facsimile. In the very twinkling of an eye.

Sadly there is a doubtless transitory drawback in the switchboard system. So – nobody knows.

He goes to the main door.

What they must think of us out there.

He goes out.

SPASSOV. I lost as well.

KAPLAN. You rode on Moscow, Victor. We rode back.

He goes out through the main doors. The lights fade to near darkness. SPASSOV stands at the window, looking out, his face illuminated by torchlight. We hear the hubbub of a large crowd.

Scene Two

In the scene change, the detritus on the tables is removed, and one of the tables itself as well. When the lights come up, therefore, an L-shaped arrangement will be left. But for the moment, we stay in darkness, apart from the torchlight. It is a week later. Still the crowd. SPASSOV stands at the window. PRUS' voice through the darkness.

PRUS. Now, you know the rule. As long as they're in the street they're a queue. They hit the square, they're a mob.

SPASSOV turns and smiles. PRUS comes to the window, looks out.

Aha.

Slight pause.

Oh, and apparently the Kremlin called.

SPASSOV. They did? What for?

PRUS. They want us to invade.

SPASSOV gets it. Then:

SPASSOV. So what's the news?

PRUS. They cannot find the duty electrician.

SPASSOV. Ah, well. The limits of command economies.

PRUS. Or any candles. Or a working torch.

SPASSOV. Well, ditto.

PRUS. And with just one matter to resolve. And the old can go, and usher in the new.

Slight pause.

I think that Kaplan's rather looking forward to it, really. Keeps going on about the flag beneath his arm.

Pause. SPASSOV looks out of the window.

SPASSOV. In fact, there were no good Marxist arguments against the phasing out of the centralised economy. Indeed we argued that cooperatives, self-management and so on were in fact more appropriate forms for socialist productive enterprises in a modern technological society.

PRUS. You did.

SPASSOV. The class struggle had been won. The pressing task was to develop the economy. There was a clear and vital role for specialists.

PRUS. Of course.

SPASSOV. We even had proposals to create an opposition party. It didn't seem that there was any scientific reason why two parties should not coexist within a pluralistic socialist society. No argument was seriously advanced against it.

PRUS. No?

SPASSOV. Or indeed against the notion of a democratically and universally elected President.

Pause.

PRUS. Victor, nobody disputes –

SPASSOV. And of course there were mistakes and contradictions. God knows, there were adventurists and opportunists in our ranks. But I still consider what has happened now to be because of not despite what happened then.

Pause.

PRUS. Victor, I quite agree. And I know of nobody who doesn't.

SPASSOV. And of course today you do have certain geopolitical advantages.

PRUS. As everyone acknowledges.

SPASSOV. Like not having 100,000 of your ally's soldiers in your streets.

PRUS. Of course.

SPASSOV. Which is why it's hurtful to be told that one's no more than Stalin's grin.

Pause.

PRUS. Victor, these people were in jail. For writing things and saying things, quite often things which started very properly with an acknowledgement of the importance of New Morning. And God knows being put in jail doesn't guarantee your virtue, and it may do quite precisely the reverse. But they went through it, and you didn't. And human nature being what it is, that influences how they – how we – think about these matters now we're out of jail and about to join the government.

SPASSOV. I'm not sure they know what we did go through.

PRUS. It's difficult to know what anybody goes through. Didn't Lutz and Kaplan first meet in a concentration camp?

Slight pause.

SPASSOV. In fact –

PRUS. It's just the fact you never signed.

SPASSOV. I wasn't always asked.

PRUS. Oh, you were asked enough.

SPASSOV. And it seemed always to be pop groups.

PRUS. So, what's wrong with pop groups?

SPASSOV. And I suppose essentially I always saw these cultural and artistic questions as a secondary –

PRUS. Yes. You did. Whereas we saw them as essentially primary. We didn't see the way out in draft programmes, action plans or even manifestoes. But as people living out their lives as if they were free people. On the eccentrically utopian assumption that if you do that long enough, then reality will eventually catch up. As it did of course on the 18th of November, when those kids stuck flowers behind policemen's shields, sang Beatles and Bob Dylan songs, and did it in the road.

SPASSOV. Well, nobody disagrees –

PRUS. And then a week ago, when I was at a Platform plenary – a *plenary* – and we were formulating or revising or amending – as it happens I think 'sharpening' – a resolution on some topic or another, suddenly, the doors flew open and a group of kids burst in dressed as Young Pioneers. Blue blouses and red kerchiefs. Shorts. The lot. And they announced themselves to be a Special Operations Unit of the Central Ministerial Commission for the Rooting Out of Self-Importance and nobody was to move. And they gave us all these small round plastic mirrors, in which we were enjoined to watch out for the tell-tale signs that We were turning into Them.

SPASSOV. That's charming.

PRUS. Well, it was very 60s. Western journalists were quite appalled.

SPASSOV. My 60s weren't quite like that.

PRUS. No. And you can still say 'pressing tasks' and 'contradiction' and 'adventurist' and keep a more or less straight face.

SPASSOV. Can I? Can I really?

PRUS. Or even, 'pluralistic socialist society'.

Slight pause.

And of course there should be a democratically elected President, and Parliament, with independent parties, even maybe three or four. But as you know, the proposition at the moment is that these good things can't happen all at once, and that the President should be appointed, for the moment, by the National Assembly. And that God help us all it should be me.

Slight pause.

I am regarded as symbolic of a clean break with the past.

SPASSOV. As opposed to a reminder of a national humiliation.

PRUS. No, I didn't mean that.

SPASSOV. You know you cannot run this country without people who were leading cadres in the party.

PRUS. There are several former leading cadres who are being most supportive.

SPASSOV. You can't put everyone who isn't up for trial.

PRUS. We're putting hardly anybody up for trial. But those we are, we must. Including the man who expelled you from the party, and who has for nearly 20 years preached water and drunk wine.

SPASSOV. And who as you point out, spent his late teens in Buchenwald.

Pause. PRUS *changes tack.*

PRUS. There's a fairy story, well a genre. You will know it well. There's a family, a peasant and his wife, who are living in great poverty and shame. And a witch or fairy comes along and offers them three wishes. But because they fail to think it through, they waste the first wish on something trivial, they do something silly and bad-tempered with the second, and they have to use the third to put things back to where they were. And you always think, if they'd been really smart, their first wish would have been that all their other wishes would come true. But in fact of course wishes never work like that. They all have unintended drawbacks. And that's the whole point of the story.

Slight pause.

At root it's the same myth as the genie in the bottle, or the book in the forbidden room, or Pandora's Box, or the serpent's apple. The spirit with his promises of boundless power who once unleashed turns out to be a demon.

Pause.

SPASSOV. So what have you unleashed?

PRUS. Oh, something very ancient.

SPASSOV. Yes?

PRUS. The urge to be in Europe once again.

SPASSOV. A Europe capitalist or socialist?

PRUS. I hope a Europe where you can't say either of those words without putting on a funny voice.

SPASSOV. All right. A Europe Swedish or American?

PRUS. Ah. The enticing Swedish Model. Have you ever been?

SPASSOV. Not for some years. But when I was there, it did seem preferable to New York or Chicago. And now I'm told there's the equivalent of our whole population unemployed in Western Europe, and every major city's full of people sleeping under bits of cardboard in the street.

PRUS. Yes, the trouble is that the alternative to some people sleeping in the streets at night is everybody sleeping indoors through the day. As a factory manager remarked, there was no unemployment in the socialist republic, so all of them were in his auto-plant instead.

SPASSOV *gives a little smile.*

The state gives people what they need. Not what they want.

SPASSOV. And that is?

PRUS (*with a shrug*). Freedom.

SPASSOV. To, or from?

PRUS. Well, not from coke or Burger King.

SPASSOV. But perhaps from fear.

PRUS. Oh, you don't think there was fear –

SPASSOV. And insecurity.

PRUS. Well, once again –

SPASSOV. From the sense that if you're not a young and thrusting sort of chap, if in fact you're old or weak or frail, then you're alone.

Surrounded by a bleak indifferent world. And that if things go bad
for you then no-one's going to care.

PRUS. What you mean, like they care now?

SPASSOV. Because –

Suddenly, a torch beams through the small door. MONICA FREIE *comes
into the room. She locates the telephone. She goes to it and dials. She doesn't
see* PRUS *or* SPASSOV.

FREIE Hi there. Now, look, I haven't got much time.
No there's been a drawback in the meeting. Lights have gone. No,
not a power cut. Apparently, a failure in the building.
You are about the 20th person to say that. Now, look –
No, dear, we've got direct lines now. With the compliments of Messrs
Siemens of West Germany. Now, listen here –
Well, it's hardly of the greatest possible importance, but as it
happens it's a working party of a sub-committee of the new
Commission into Parliamentary Procedures. For which I'm taking
notes and handing round the liquid tarmac. And yes in many ways
it's very much the same but at least thank God a little lighter on the
heroic toilers of the world so there's rather less about the urgent
need to further double and redouble efforts to complete the tasks
set by the 14th Congress.

Enjoying herself:

Or welcoming a letter from a hundred workers at the Glorious
October Valve and Lightbulb Factory protesting at the latest crude
attempt by the lackeys of US Imperialism to whip up infantile
delusions among petit-bourgeois elements.

Responding:

Or indeed their foiled attempts to weaken anti-fascist vigilance.

Responding:

Or you bet the dreadful things they do to Negroes.
Whereas the only links I'm bothered with at this historic juncture are
the ones I forge with you. Now you'll recall I told you I'm a fortnight
late -

The lights come up.

Ah. Light. Well, anyway -

The phone goes dead.

Oh, shit. Hallo. Hallo?

PRUS. Hallo.

FREIE *turns and sees* PRUS *and* SPASSOV.

Please, carry on.

FREIE. Uh, actually . . . In fact, the line . . . Uh, no.

She puts the phone down. She goes quickly out. PRUS *smiles.*

SPASSOV. I once signed a letter. In the early 50s. I was one of 17 young
cadres of the Friedrich Engels Anti-Fascist Shock Brigade.
Demanding the immediate expulsion from the party of fifth
columnists and self-styled Titoites. And after I was expelled, Lutz
reprinted it in the Star to demonstrate the full depths of my
opportunism. Having been of course a self-styled Titoite himself.

KAPLAN *comes in through the small door.*

KAPLAN. Ah here you are. We had in fact found candles. There's been
quite a run on them in recent days. But one hopes no longer.

PRUS. Well, yes, certainly.

KAPLAN *goes and looks out of the window at the procession. Then he turns
back.*

KAPLAN. We should perhaps restart as soon as possible. There's very
little to resolve.

He picks up a look from SPASSOV. *He is going; he turns back.*

An incident, apparently. A young Vietnamese. Guest worker, walking
to his dormitory. And rather badly beaten, by a gang of young men
with short hair.

Slight pause.

And the first graffiti. Gas All Gypsies Now.

Slight pause.

So when you're ready, – gentlemen.

He goes out.

SPASSOV. In fact, they weren't in the same camp. Lutz was political,
and sent to Buchenwald. But if you were 13 and a Jew in 1943 you got
sent straight to Birkenau. It's a miracle that he survived.

He goes to the window and looks out.

The voices whispering in simple people's ears. The people who felt
safe before. The demons that we're letting loose. And indeed the

Europe we're rejoining.

He turns back to PRUS.

Please convey to the Committee my support – my warm support – for the immediate election of the President by the members of the National Assembly.

He goes out through the main doors.

Scene Three

A fortnight later. Now all has been removed except one table, pushed to the side, and a single chair. On the table is laid an overcoat and scarf, belonging to JOSEF LUTZ, *who sits on the chair. He wears a suit and no tie. Both doors are shut. A moment or two.* LUTZ *stands, goes to the window and looks out. We might expect that someone will come through the main doors, but in fact we hear a slight rattle of keys from the small door.* PRUS *enters, looking oddly formal in a dark suit and striped tie.·*

PRUS. So then. 'In here'.

LUTZ. Ah. Mr President.

PRUS. Not for at least an hour. The chaps assure me I could still be quite conclusively assassinated.

LUTZ. Or asphyxiated.

PRUS. What?

LUTZ. Aren't you being blessed or something? By that geriatric Cardinal?

PRUS. Yes, I am. And me a registered asthmatic. Don't tell me there's a demonstration calling for my overthrow already.

He goes to see what LUTZ *is looking at out of the window.*

LUTZ. Not yet. In fact, I'm looking at myself. In prison for some reason mirrors are in short supply. But luckily, in dirty glass . . .

He turns to PRUS.

Free market. And already we've a shortage of skilled window-cleaners. Can't think why.

PRUS *smiles.* LUTZ *is looking at him carefully.*

PRUS. Don't tell me. I look quite ridiculous.

He notices a dirty mark on his jacket. Trying to scratch it off:

My mother used to say, Pavel looks good in anything he eats.

He takes out a packet of cigarettes.

D'you want a cigarette?

LUTZ. I'm trying to give it up.

PRUS (*lighting up*). Wish I could. So, how's jail?

LUTZ. I'd forgotten how good it was, not having to pretend.

PRUS. Yes. Yes, I used to like that too.

Slight pause.

And I can't pretend I've very long.

He takes a paper from his pocket.

You're charged with treason, corruption, abuse of authority and running an unconstitutional organisation.

LUTZ. Yes.

PRUS. We're going to drop the treason.

LUTZ. Thanks.

PRUS. And corruption insofar as it's not covered by abuse.

LUTZ. Well, ditto.

PRUS. And the last charge we're told won't stand up.

LUTZ. Why not?

PRUS. Apparently, unconstitutional. So we're left with abusing the authority of a public official.

LUTZ. Hardly worth it really.

PRUS. That's what we thought too.

He hands LUTZ *the paper.*

So all we need is a single sentence letter on those lines. Well, in those words.

LUTZ. Please Mr Prus I'm sorry pardon me.

PRUS. Well, more or less.

LUTZ. And if I don't?

PRUS. You go on trial. But it's an academic question, surely.

  LUTZ *goes and puts the letter on the table near his coat.*

LUTZ. I wonder, who I have to thank for this.

  PRUS *shrugs.* LUTZ *sits.*

  Who else?

PRUS. Oh, quite a few. We're charging Kubat, Skuratov and Ledl.

LUTZ. Vladislav?

PRUS. No evidence he took a penny.

LUTZ. He was working for a foreign power.

PRUS. He was working in the interests of a foreign power. As were you. We may insist on a percentage of his royalties.

LUTZ. His what?

PRUS. He's signed a contract with a prominent West German publisher.

LUTZ. And Milev I gather back in favour in a big way.

PRUS. I think many people are impressed by how he's cleaning up the party.

LUTZ. Whatever it's called now.

PRUS. The Democratic Socialists.

LUTZ. And is the rumour true it's running driving schools?

PRUS. And a chauffeur service from the airport. Well, you had a lot of cars.

LUTZ. So what about the buildings? Gaming houses? Brothels? Or a Stock Exchange?

PRUS. I think they'll be appropriated by the people. Particularly when they're weekend cottages, hunting lodges, and private sanatoria.

LUTZ. Oh, and of course, there's never any question of that kind of thing on your side. Young Zietek, swanning off to Washington on student funds to speak at right-wing congresses and taking skiing holidays in Maine. Or did the Western papers get it wrong?

PRUS. It was not accurately reported.

LUTZ. Oh. Oh, *dear*.

PRUS. But it was not a prudent thing to do.

LUTZ. I'm told by people who fly aeroplanes that taking off is really not that hard. The tricky thing is getting it back down again. As you will find. In many many ways.

PRUS. Name some.

LUTZ. Well, for a start, light cracks about assassination. And of course it's true, the world is dangerous, and it doesn't let up at weekends. And your chaps inform you frankly it's much easier for them if instead of popping down the road to see your doctor she pops up to you. And they'd sooner honestly if that applied to haircuts, restaurants and basic daily purchasing as well. And when you've Bush or Thatcher and no doubt the President of General Motors dropping by to chew the fat on points of common interest, then of course they have to eat, and if they're going to be shot by terrorists, it's generally felt that all in all it would be better done in someone else's country. And before you know it you are living in the lap of luxury behind a 12 foot wire and the people look at you and those you have replaced and they can't tell the difference.

Pause.

PRUS. The difference being, surely, that the people would be told. And if they didn't like it then they could get rid of you. In something under 40 years. The difference is, the state would not be built on people lying all the time. But of course I take the point.

Slight pause.

In fact, the other week, a gang of kids dressed up of all things as Young Pioneers -

LUTZ. I saw this room, first, on the 12th of April 1945. I was with a group of national partisans who like me had joined the party when they frankly didn't hand out prizes for it, and that day we occupied this palace, till that day the HQ of the Nazi so-called civilian administration. And as you might imagine, having smashed things up a bit, we fell to raising flags, and striking attitudes, and proclaiming futures of an unimaginable scale and splendour, in which the immense and boundless untapped energies and talents of the masses would be liberated, every peasant would be Aristotle, every worker Michelangelo.

If you like, we'd write the last line of the story of mankind. The modest sort of fellows that we were. And where everyone had got it wrong, we'd get it finally, and unalterably right.

And this room had obviously been some sort of ballroom, because all the walls were covered with great mirrors in gilt frames. And so we stood here, in our working blouses and red armbands, and we swore that if we ever looked into a mirror and we couldn't recognise ourselves that day, then we'd tear up our party cards and descend into oblivion.

Pause.

You see, it wasn't that the working class weren't up to it. It was that we weren't up to it. We weren't betrayed by saboteurs. We didn't need to be. It was pilot error. Nothing wrong with the machine. And I've often thought, thank God they took those mirrors down.

Long pause.

I'm sorry. You were saying. People dressed up as Young Pioneers.

Pause. PRUS *shrugs, as if to say, 'It doesn't matter now'. Enter* BRODSKAYA *up the stairs.*

BRODSKAYA. Mr Prus, we really ought to go.

PRUS. Of course.

BRODSKAYA *tightens* PRUS' *tie.*

BRODSKAYA. You have your speech?

PRUS. I have my speech.

BRODSKAYA. You'll need your overcoat. It's very cold.

PRUS. Right then.

A moment, then BRODSKAYA *goes out.*

LUTZ. Ah. The trials of being Head of State.

PRUS. You know, I think you're wrong. I don't think it's a failure of example. Honestly. I don't think it's anything to do with individuals at all.

LUTZ. Well, that's good Marxist thinking.

PRUS. Do you know the real slogan of this revolution? If you can call it that, with not a window broken?

LUTZ. Yet. No, tell me.

PRUS. 'Back to normal'. Communism, one of those appalling holidays you read about, where some mad enthusiastic schoolteacher takes a group of pupils up a mountain, and when the weather turns, he can't cope and the whole thing ends in tears. The message of our revolution: Please, no more adventures. No more heroism. Certainly, no more unimaginably splendid futures. Just: let's get back to the normal, ordinary way of doing things. The way that works. The way they do them in the west.

LUTZ. So that's what you're going to tell them? No more fairy tales? No more grand stories? Back to normal?

PRUS. It is – what they want.

LUTZ. For now.

BRODSKAYA *has re-entered with* PRUS' *overcoat.*

BRODSKAYA. Uh, Mr Prus . . . I'm told the Guard of Honour's threatening a putsch.

PRUS. Yes. Yes.

PRUS *takes a pen from his pocket and puts it on the table near the document.*

PRUS. There is a car to take you to a villa. For a week or two. And I suppose the person that you have to thank is Victor Spassov. And, yes, that is exactly what I'm going to try and tell them.

He takes his coat and goes out with BRODSKAYA *through the small door. Pause.* LUTZ *goes and looks at the document. He picks up the pen. He puts it in his pocket. He goes to the window and looks out. Suddenly, a key turns in the main doors, they open, and* MONICA FREIE *enters. She sees* LUTZ *at the window.*

FREIE. Excuse me.

LUTZ. What? Oh. Yes.

FREIE *takes the keys from the main door.*

FREIE. I've come to take you to your car.

LUTZ. My car.

FREIE. And apparently, there is a document.

LUTZ. Yes. yes, there is.

LUTZ *goes to the document.* FREIE *goes towards the small door.*

FREIE. It's waiting round the back. In 12th of April St. Though they call it something different now.

LUTZ. I see.

Slight pause.

So then, they kept you on.

FREIE. Yes. Yes, the President . . .

LUTZ. Of course. D'you have a cigarette?

FREIE. Of course.

Finding the pack:

In fact, I'd hoped to give up working altogether. But it didn't work out quite that way. A – false alarm.

LUTZ. I'm sorry.

FREIE (*offering a cigarette*). There you are.

LUTZ. Well, thanks.

As LUTZ *takes the cigarette.*

FREIE. The Western press all think it's very odd. How much we all still smoke.

LUTZ. And do you have a light?

FREIE. Yes, certainly.

She takes out her Marlboro lighter. She remembers PRUS *and the matches.*

Um, I . . .

She shrugs, and puts down the lighter. LUTZ *puts the cigarette in his mouth, stands, goes to the table, picks up the document, lights the lighter. Then he lets it go out, puts down the document, turns, goes back and gives the lighter and the cigarette to* FREIE.

LUTZ. Just tell yourself, it's either them or you.

FREIE. Yes. Right.

Pause. As LUTZ *is making no move, she doesn't know quite what to do. So she goes over to the document.*

FREIE. The driver says you're going to the country.

LUTZ. Yes.

FREIE. And this is, uh, the document?

LUTZ. That's right.

FREIE. Um, Comrade Lutz . . .

LUTZ. Yes, what?

Slight pause.

FREIE. It's just, if you'll forgive me saying . . .

LUTZ. Yes?

FREIE. It's just, I think it's right that they're not putting you on trial. I mean, whatever drawbacks and shortcomings there were with the system. It isn't right that individuals should take the blame.

LUTZ. You really think that?

FREIE. Yes I do. 'Cause after all, it's not as if, it was like that dreadful thing in China.

Slight pause.

LUTZ. No.

FREIE *looks at the document. She realises the problem.*

FREIE. Oh heavens. Didn't they leave you a pen?

She is looking for a pen in her pocket.

LUTZ. They did. But I don't think I'll have need of it.

She looks at him.

I mean, no gestures. No heroic conflagrations. Nothing grand.

Slight pause. He goes and picks up the document.

But I was in at the beginning. And, whatever errors and mistakes have been committed, I think all in all it's best if I'm still in it at the end.

We begin to hear bells ringing for the inauguration of the President. LUTZ folds the document once and tears it across. He goes and takes the keys from FREIE, goes to the main doors, locks them, and takes the keys back to FREIE.

Please say I'm sorry to the driver.

More bells join. LUTZ picks up his coat and scarf. He sits on the chair. After a moment, FREIE goes out through the small door. By now bells are tolling all round the theatre. LUTZ sits, his scarf and coat across his knees.

Lights fade.

End of play